D1589229

TEXTILE TREASURES

AT THE
GLASGOW
SCHOOL
OF ART

WITHDRAWN

LIVERPOOL JOHN MOORES UNIVERSITY
Aldham Roberts L.R.C.
TEL. 0151 231 3701/3634

LIVERPOOL JMU LIBRARY

3   1111   01123   8274

TEXTILE TREASURES

AT THE GLASGOW SCHOOL OF ART

LIZ ARTHUR

THE GLASGOW SCHOOL OF ART PRESS
in conjunction with
THE HERBERT PRESS • LONDON
an imprint of A&C Black

First published 2005 for
The Glasgow School of Art Press
by The Herbert Press (an imprint of A&C Black)
37 Soho Square
London W1D 3QZ
www.acblack.com

ISBN-10: 0-7136-7188-2
ISBN-13: 978-0-7136-7188-9

© 2005 Liz Arthur

A CIP record for this title is available from the British Library.

Liz Arthur has asserted her rights under the Copyright, Design and Patents Act, 1988, to be identified as the author of this work.

All rights reserved. No part of this publication may be reproduced in any form or by any means – graphic, electronic or mechanical, including photocopying, recording, taping or information storage and retrieval systems – without the prior permission in writing of the publishers.

Jacket designed by Sutchinda Thompson
Book designed by Peter Bailey

Front cover:
Top row (l to r): Handkerchief sachet designed by Rebecca Crompton, 1938; Fragment of embroidery, early 18th century; Detail of teacloth, possibly Danish, 20th century. Middle row (l to r): Panel designed and worked by Margaret Macdonald Mackintosh; Detail, dragon robe, 19th century. Bottom row (l to r): Detail of woman's shawl, Punjab, early 20th century; 'Carnival' panel designed and worked by Molly Booker, 1937; 'Little Visitor' by Kathleen Mann, mid 1930s.

Back cover:
Cushion cover designed by Jessie Newbery and worked by Edith Rowat, 1890s; Decorative animal by Shirley Tweedale, 1959; Man's waistcoat, late 18th century.

Printed and bound in China by C & C Offset Printing Co. Ltd.

A&C Black uses paper produced with elemental chlorine-free pulp, harvested from managed sustainable sources.

Acknowledgements

A major debt of gratitude is due to Sandra Heffernan of Massey University, New Zealand, whose recent research for her PhD, 'Design from Artefacts: Innovate or Imitate: Issues of Aesthetics, Education, Collecting, Making and Marketing in Coats' Needlework Development Scheme: 1934–1962' has been of great help in compiling this book. This, the first major study of the subject, is especially important for Glasgow School of Art's textile archive. Her work on the German, Austrian and Hungarian embroideries contributes enormously to our understanding of their significance. In addition, her discovery that, in several instances, work identified as Mexican or Hungarian are copies worked in Coats' studios using Coats' thread is of particular importance to curators of all Needlework Development Scheme collections in museums.

The following Glasgow School of Art staff have provided invaluable assistance: first and foremost Sarah Hepworth, archivist, whose help and advice are much appreciated; Lorna McParland, Visual Communications Department and Sharon McPake, library technician, for most of the textile images; Peter Trowles, Curator of the Mackintosh Collection who provided archival photographs and George Rawson, Fine Art Librarian, whose encyclopaedic knowledge of the School's history is always so generously shared. Thanks also to Kathryn Howell of Glasgow School of Art Enterprises. In addition, Anne Ellis, former curator of Hill House, shared her thoughts on Margaret Macdonald Mackintosh's panels and Anne Ferguson information on knitted items. Every effort has been made to contact private owners and thanks are due to all those who have given permission to use images, particularly Glasgow Museums and Margot Sandeman for permission to use the photograph of her mother Muriel Boyd. Finally thanks to Anne Watts for editorial help and to Linda Lambert of A. & C. Black at whose instigation this book has been written.

Contents

LIVERPOOL JOHN MOORES UNIVERSITY
LEARNING SERVICES

Entrance to Charles
Rennie Mackintosh's
Glasgow School of Art
from the first phase,
1897–99; the building
was completed in
1909 and continues to
function as a working
School.

Introduction

Textile Design at Glasgow School of Art

The Glasgow School of Art Study Centre was established in 2001 to house the textile archive within the Charles Rennie Mackintosh building, combining separate collections of textile work from GSA departments since the 19th century, from the Needlework Development Scheme (1934–1962) and from individual donors. It has always been valuable, indeed essential, to have examples available to students for reference and inspiration. However, these were not only examples of work done at GSA or by its students, but pieces of older work and from many different countries which enabled the study of a wider range of techniques and design.

To facilitate an understanding of the diverse collection, a brief history of its development is provided in this Introduction. There is an explanation of the significance of particular groups of items within the development and of their relationship to some of the influential individuals who have shaped the teaching of embroidery at GSA.

The Introduction is followed by illustrations of a selection of individual examples, chosen not only to show some of the most important items, but also to give an idea of the breadth of the collection.

Textiles have been inextricably linked with GSA since its opening as one of the Government-sponsored Schools of Design in January 1845. It was one of a number of such Branch Schools set up under the control of the South Kensington Institution (that then included what became the Victoria and Albert Museum and the Royal College of Art), as a direct result of the House of Commons Select Committee on Arts and Manufactures of 1835–36, in order to address the problem of poor design in Britain. At that time Glasgow and the West of Scotland were a major textile-producing area with the manufacture of cotton; weaving and printing of shawls, not only in Paisley but also in Glasgow; the Turkey red industry in the Vale of Leven as well as other aspects of the trade. Consequently the first management committee of the School included a calico printer, a manufacturer of DeLaine (a soft woollen fabric), two shawl

1

LIVERPOOL JOHN MOORES UNIVERSITY
LEARNING SERVICES

makers, an upholsterer and a sewed-muslin manufacturer. From the outset, design for textiles was seen as important. Indeed the Lord Provost of Glasgow Sir James Campbell suggested in 1843 that the setting-up of a design school would raise the standard of patterns for linen and cotton and flowered muslin as well as for carpets and wallpapers. However, although the Schools of Design trained draughtsmen, they failed to produce original designers or make any impact on industrial design; French designers continued to predominate. For example, J. C. Wakefield, a Glasgow silk manufacturer, explained to a Parliamentary commission on design in 1849 that, although he had five or six designers, he himself decided which parts of designs to put together. He bought most of his designs from Paris as he considered the French designers 'a much higher class of men than they are in this country, they are more respectable.'

Ann Macbeth and Fra Newbery in a drawing and painting class, c1911–12

The Schools of Design came under the control of the Science and Art Department at South Kensington which ran a national curriculum of art instruction with a national competition held annually. Success in the competition was crucial to the School's funding as the number of awards given to each institution directly influenced the size of the grant awarded. Although Glasgow was moderately successful, the appointment of Francis H. Newbery (1855–1946) in 1885 brought radical changes that led Glasgow School of Art to become the most successful in Britain between 1898 and 1901, winning more national awards and medals than any other School. It also gained international acclaim. Newbery's commitment to the teaching of design was central to that transformation and his energy, enthusiasm, determination and ambition created a dynamic environment that allowed individual talent to flourish.

It must be remembered that Glasgow was not a backwater in the 19th century, but a thriving industrial city known as the 'second city of the British Empire'. It hosted major international exhibitions in 1888 and 1901 (and later in 1911 and 1938), and there was a lively art scene with the 'Glasgow Boys' group of painters at its centre. The Glasgow Institute of Fine Arts, a private exhibiting society, was founded in 1861 and its own purpose-built galleries in Sauchiehall Street opened in 1901. The Glasgow Art Club was founded in 1867 and the Glasgow Society of Lady Artists, the first of its kind in Scotland, in 1882. The city was also home to many wealthy industrialists who became patrons and collectors, among them Archibald McLellan (1797–1854), a coach builder whose bequest formed the basis for the municipal fine art collection and William Burrell (1861–1958), a shipowner who later bequeathed his large and diverse collection to the city. The lively reputation of the city must have attracted Newbery and the School's reputation grew under his direction.

In 1899, financial control of Glasgow School of Art passed from South Kensington to the Scottish Education Department and authority was granted to the Governors to appoint professors in Architecture, Painting, Sculpture and Design. The only other British school of art permitted to appoint professors was the Royal College of Art. As the reputation of the School grew many key design figures accepted invitations to the School. During the 1880s, Walter Crane was a frequent visitor who lectured at the School, the Glasgow Art Club and the Glasgow Socialists Society, as did William Morris and Lewis F. Day. C. F. A. Voysey was almost appointed as Professor of Design in 1908 and Jacob Epstein and M. H. Baillie Scott were considered for posts, an indication that the School had achieved real prominence in the quality and originality of the work being done. The School also hosted performances such as masques and in the lecture theatre public readings were given by Lillie Langtry and Bram Stoker, author of *Dracula*, who was Henry Irving's theatrical manager. Stoker endowed a prize in 1903 that is still awarded annually for the most imaginative work of the session.

Fra Newbery, as he liked to be known, established a diploma course in Applied Design. Before studying a craft discipline, students had first to reach a required standard in Drawing, Still Life, Painting and Modelling. The craft courses were based on the French *atelier* system, i.e. a practical training within a studio environment under the tuition of an accomplished artist/teacher. Newbery set up new technical studios in the 1890s based on Walter Crane's work at South Kensington in the 1880s where Newbery himself had taught prior to taking up his post in Glasgow. However, unusually for the time, women came to dominate the teaching of applied art in Glasgow. Among the designers educated in these technical studios and appointed as instructors were Jessie M. King (book decoration), Helen Muir Wood (enamelling and block cutting), De Courcy Lewthwaite Dewar (enamelling), Dorothy Carleton Smyth (sgraffito and gesso) and Agnes Harvey (metalwork). In Scotland women were denied university education until 1892; many middle-class women attended art schools as an alternative. They benefited from Newbery's inclusive belief in the encouragement of all individuals including women.

The Embroidery and Needlework Department, 1894-1920

One talented student, Jessie Rowat (1864–1948), married Newbery in 1889. She became Head of the first embroidery studio in 1894 and began a radical course in Art Needlework that created new aesthetic standards for embroidery through honest simplicity of design and sound craft practice. Of all the technical studios, Embroidery

3

LIVERPOOL JOHN MOORES UNIVERSITY
LEARNING SERVICES

Jessie and Fra Newbery in 'fancy dress', c1900

established an international reputation and continued to influence needlework education into the 1970s. Students studied Flowers from Nature, Design and Application, and Technique and Study of Old Examples, with drawing an essential skill that under-pinned everything. However, the study of examples from the past was not done in imitation but as a means of understanding techniques and of learning how to apply them. The embroidery studio's inception marks the beginning of the textile archive as a source for study, but few pieces available at that time survive and it is quite likely that small collections of historical needlework were borrowed from South Kensington and from Mrs Newbery's own collection.

Mrs Newbery's main aim, to encourage and devel-op the individual skills of each student, was a break with the prevalent belief that laborious execution was more important than originality.

As embroidered textiles began to play an important part in artistic unified designs for interiors, most of her work was in the form of practical items of which the mantel border (fig. 23) and cush-ion cover (fig. 24) are typical early examples. Initially, she worked in crewel wools on linen in the Arts and Crafts needlework tradition, but in lighter tones more suited to the light airy interiors being advocated by Charles Rennie Mackintosh and Voysey. However, she was insistent that embroidery should be a creative form available to all social classes and that it could be worked just as effectively on cheap, readily available materials such as hessian, calico and flannel as on expensive silk. She supported her husband's view that 'Picture painting is for the few but beauty in the com-mon surroundings of our daily lives is, or should be, an absolute necessity to the many.'[1] For her, design was of primary importance and she preferred simple stitches. Appliqué, the method of applying a fabric shape to a ground fabric became a favourite technique closely identified with the Department. She normally used linen shapes secured with satin stitch, which gave strength and solidity to the design with the additional benefit of being practical and hard-wearing on func-tional items such as portières (door curtains), bedstead hangings, table covers, bags and cushions. Another tech-

Flower drawing class, c1900

nique which she exploited was needleweaving, often used as a border for inscriptions, for which she developed her own distinctive simple lettering that contrasted with the twisting curves of the plant form (fig. 25). She had seen this technique while on a tour of Italy with an uncle, prior to attending the School of Art. Her designs were based on a life-long interest in botany and plants. Although she used plants in a simplified, stylised, almost geometric form, they retain the essence of the plant. She fostered an essentially linear style that was no doubt enhanced by her studies and designs for stained glass and mosaics. Distinctive motifs of stylised flowers, birds, butterflies and insects were part of a visual language common to all the decorative arts produced at the School.

Her work soon attracted the attention of *The Studio* which regularly featured work by her students. In an article in 1898, she expressed her radical views:

> I believe in education consisting of seeing the best that has been done. Then, having this high standard before us, in doing what we like to do: *that* for our fathers, *this* for us.
>
> I believe that nothing is common or unclean; that the design of a pepper pot is as important, in its degree, as the conception of a cathedral.
>
> I believe that material, space and consequent use discover their own exigencies and as such have to be considered well ..... I like the opposition of straight lines to curved; of horizontal to vertical; of purple to green, of green to blue ...... I specially aim at beautiful spaces and try to make them as important as the patterns.
>
> I try to make most appearance with least effort, but insist that what work is ventured on is as perfect as may be.[2]

Within a short time her original approach set new standards of both design and execution and the work produced by students gained widespread recognition. A review notice of 1902 stated:

> Look to the Glasgow School of Art if we wish to think of today's embroidery as a thing that lives and grows and is therefore of greater value and interest than a display of archaeology in patterns and stitches.[3]

Mrs Newbery, like so many other women in artistic circles, also expressed her individuality and artistic ideas in dress that was appropriate for the new artistic interiors. Others included Margaret Macdonald Mackintosh and her sister Frances MacNair whose photographs appeared in Anna Muthesius' book on artistic dress *Das Eigenkleid der Frau*. Many architects and designers, such as Walter Crane and William Morris, designed aesthetic dress as did the Viennese designers of the Wiener Werkstatte and in

1905 Liberty of London produced a handsome fashion catalogue of artistic garments shown in appropriate interiors. The following year in an article discussing Glasgow's decorative art, John Taylor said:

> Even feminine attire has not escaped the attention of the modern artist; with some recent schemes of decoration he has indicated the design and colour of the gowns to be worn, so that no disturbing element might mar the unity of the conception.'[4]

ENTWÜRFE FÜR KINDERKLEIDCHEN von R. JESSIE NEWBERY GLASGOW.

Moderne Stickereien, 1905, p. 57 showing Jessie Newbery's designs for children's dresses. Photographs of her two daughters wearing similar dresses appeared in *Das Eigenkleid der Frau* (Krefeld, 1903), written by Anna Muthesius.

Mrs Newbery's style derived from the dress reform movements of the 1880s, viz. the aesthetic movement inspired by classical drapery and medieval sculpture and rational dress that advocated freedom from restrictive corsets, heavy fabrics, tight bodices and sleeves. She wore softly gathered fabrics, most often silk velvets or lightweight wool, decorated with embroidered collars, cuff and belts that invariably incorporated functional elements as part of the design. For example, buttonholes by which a collar was fastened to the neck of the dress were emphasised by bold stitching and decorative buttons, and hems instead of being worked unobtrusively were turned to the right side and secured with bold French knots. She added texture in the form of couched thread and fine braid as well as flat beads of glass and shell. She made similar clothes for her two daughters and several designs were included in the German periodical *Moderne Stickereien*, published in Darmstadt between 1903–09.

Many other Glasgow artists designed their own clothes. In addition, Newbery's style of dress was emulated by many of her colleagues and students. For example, the collar by Grace Melvin (fig. 31) and dress by Daisy McGlashan (fig. 30), both illustrate this distinctive style. The dress is in the suffragette colours, indicating the wearer's political sympathy and, indeed, many of the students, artists and designers associated with GSA at that time were supporters of the suffrage movement. Both Jessie Newbery and Ann Macbeth, and other members of the Lady Artists' Club, were members of the Women's Social and Political Union whose Scottish branch was set up in Glasgow by 1906. Jessie Newbery organised the 'Arts and Curios' stall at the Grand Suffrage Bazaar held in the St Andrew's Halls in Glasgow in 1910 and students in the Department took turns between classes to stitch banners designed by Ann Macbeth, that were intended to be carried at rallies. The banners were exhibited at the Fine Art Institute in 1908. Unfortunately none of these banners has been identified, but one banner designed by Ann Macbeth was found recently in the School (fig. 26).

Embroidery classes expanded in 1899 when the administration of the School's funding grant was taken over by the Scottish Education Department which then issued regulations for the further training of teachers. Saturday classes in embroidery for both primary and secondary school teachers were begun and after three years the students were eligible for a certificate of proficiency. Needlework, therefore, became an important element in the school curriculum throughout Glasgow and the West of Scotland. In addition, although not available to teachers, there was a two-year certificate course in Art Needlework recognised by the Scottish Education Department. Significantly the Embroidery Department was the only one within the School of Art to award an individual certificate, first issued in 1907, and to have a separate entry in the Annual Report. From a minor subject, embroidery had rapidly become the most important craft taught in the School and through the work of Ann Macbeth was to gain international recognition.

Muriel Boyd, seen here with her sister in 1906, was a student from 1906–10. She later became needlework mistress at schools in Bearsden then at Rosslyn Terrace, Glasgow.

Ann Macbeth (1875–1948), who enrolled as a student in 1897, was appointed assistant instructress to Jessie Newbery in 1901, continuing to assist until 1908 when she was appointed Head of Department on Jessie Newbery's retirement. Frances MacNair (1874–1921) worked as Macbeth's assistant from 1908 until 1911 and Mary Newbery Sturrock, the Newberys' younger daughter, believed that the most beautiful work produced in the Department was the result of MacNair's influence[5]. Certainly at that time Macbeth produced several designs with magnificent winged figures and more striking vivid colours. A talented and prolific embroiderer, Macbeth's work drew considerable attention, particularly her figure panels and in 1902 she won a silver medal at the 'Turin International Exhibition of Decorative Art'. The same year both she and Jessie Newbery were invited to exhibit in Budapest. However, her main legacy is as a teacher. She took charge of the Saturday classes for teachers from 1904 and also held classes for workers in thread mills. Through these classes she began to develop a practical method of teaching children needlework that did not lose sight of creativity. She was helped considerably by Margaret Swanson, an experienced primary school teacher who was her assistant from 1910–13.

Swanson attended classes at Glasgow School of Art and together she and Macbeth devised a method that aimed to develop the child's skill in conjunction with developing hand and eye co-ordination without repressing enthusiasm or imagination. Instead of working samples with small stitches in white thread on white fabric, as was the norm, the child made simple

Ann Macbeth wearing a collar embroidered by herself, c1900.
Photo Glasgow Museums

LIVERPOOL JOHN MOORES UNIVERSITY
LEARNING SERVICES

Margaret Swanson by
Ann Macbeth, 1910.
*Private collection, photo
Glasgow Museums*

functional articles with coloured fabrics and thread, each stage progressing logically from the previous one with increasing degrees of difficulty. This method was taught to the teachers attending the Saturday classes and a successful exhibition of their work in 1909 drew increased attention to this method. The following year samples of work were sent to the 'Thirty-sixth International Exhibition of German Art Workers and Teachers' in Hanover. Work was also exhibited in the Education Offices at London County Council and in Chester. Samples were presented to the Canadian Royal Commission on Education who visited the School. Interest increased further with the publication in 1911 of Swanson and Macbeth's *Educational Needlecraft*.

To promote this system of teaching, Ann Macbeth organised the loan of parcels of samples. Loans were requested by schools in Yorkshire, Lancashire, Cumberland, Wales, Dorset, Bedford, London, Africa, America, West Indies and India. In December 1911, an exhibition of the work was held at the School of Art and during its two weeks attracted 14,000 visitors. Representatives from various educational bodies visited Glasgow to study the new teaching method at first hand. In 1912 these included Miss Black from Chicago University, Mrs Napier from South Africa and Miss Sillitoe of the English Board of Education.

Macbeth and Swanson organised lectures and summer schools throughout Britain. Lectures on needlecraft were delivered by Ann Macbeth in Glasgow and Carlisle and by Margaret Swanson 'in Nottingham, Derby and London to the Froebel Society, at Sheffield at the University, at Homerton and Bingley Training Colleges and also at Bradford, Leeds and Bath, Brechin, Ayr and Helensburgh'[6]. The system was used throughout Britain from the Shetlands to the Channel Islands and worldwide from St Helena to Tasmania and New Zealand. In addition, Ann Macbeth helped devise a new course, approved by the Scottish Education Department, for the West of Scotland College of Domestic Science; in 1914, she drew up a programme of work for the National Froebel Union's proposed diploma in handwork. Both Swanson and Macbeth continued to disseminate

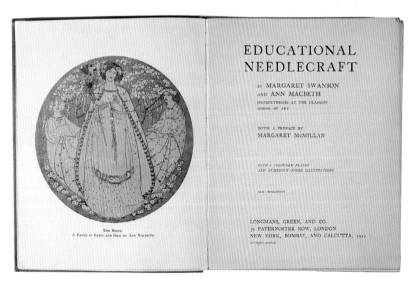

Educational Needlecraft,
title page and
frontispiece, 1911

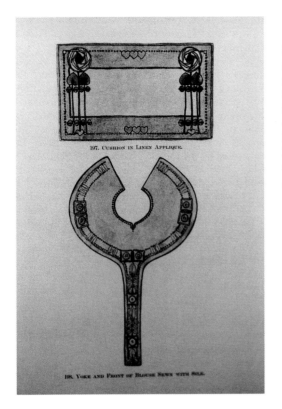

197. CUSHION IN LINEN APPLIQUE.

198. YOKE AND FRONT OF BLOUSE SEWN WITH SILK.

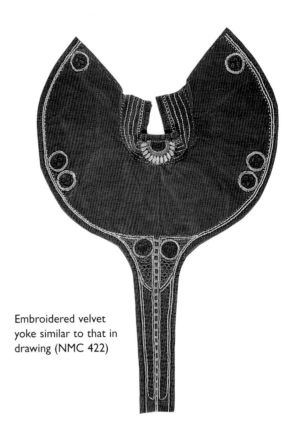

Illustration from *Educational Needlecraft*, p.115, showing yoke and front of blouse designed by Ann Macbeth from 'Lesson XVII, Designs based on a circle, Age 14–15 years'.

Embroidered velvet yoke similar to that in drawing (NMC 422)

their ideas through further books. In recognition of her work, Ann Macbeth received honorary diplomas from Paris, Ghent, Budapest and Chicago. In effect, the initiative provided by Jessie Newbery and developed by Ann Macbeth provided the foundation of modern embroidery and training of designer craftswomen.

One of the Glasgow School of Art students who also attended the Saturday classes was Grace Melvin (1890–1977). In 1912 she was awarded an excellent grade in the Needlecraft certificate and was appointed Needlecraft Mistress to the Townhead Primary School Continuation Class in Glasgow. The following year she was appointed to classes in Barrhead and acted as an instructress at the Guernsey and Scarborough Summer Schools. She continued as a day student at Glasgow School of Art studying lettering and during the First World War was commissioned to produce several roles of honour for Glasgow churches. In 1920, she was appointed as a teacher of lettering and illumination at GSA, which she continued for six years until granted a year's leave of absence to assist in the inauguration of a craft section in the Vancouver School of Art. A newspaper report of her visit described her as an 'ardent advocate of educational needlecraft' and she took the opportunity to extol its virtues[7]. She retired from GSA in 1927 and continued as Head of the Design Department in

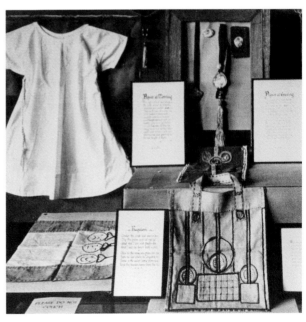

Exhibition of work by Grace Melvin at the School of Art, 1912. In addition to items from Macbeth and Swanson's teaching programme, there are examples of lettering, illumination and jewellery.

Items from Grace Melvin's exhibition in 1912. The baby coat based on *Educational Needlecraft*, p. 21 'Lesson IX, Flannel seams, Age 10–11 years'.
Photos Glasgow Museums

Vancouver until her retirement, during which time she published several books on design. After her death a collection of her needlework was returned to Glasgow and now forms a comprehensive example of Macbeth and Swanson's method which continued to be taught in Scottish Schools until the 1960s.

In 1914, the work of staff and former students was shown at the 'Arts Décoratifs de Grande Bretagne' exhibition at the Louvre, Paris, and, in the same year at Lyons, the School was represented by photographs of Charles Rennie Mackintosh's building and examples of embroidery. With the outbreak of war in Europe, the Department's students and staff became active in several war efforts. Students were commissioned by the Trades House to stitch two pairs of regimental colours for the 1st and 2nd City of Glasgow Battalions of the Highland Light Infantry for Glasgow Corporation. (These were exhibited at the School's 1916 exhibition.) In addition, they sent six large packages of comforts to soldiers and one student was sent to Reading to organise needlework as an employment for wounded soldiers. The students taught in factories and in classes for the Women's Co-operative Guilds; at the 'National Economy Exhibition' in London, 1916, embroideries from the School were shown illustrating 'how cheap clothes might be beautiful with dainty stitchery and artistic application of colour'[8]. In addition, staff in the School's decorative art studios suggested holding a major exhibition to raise funds for Belgian refugees and the Scottish branch of the Red Cross. The students organised a 'Tryst' with a variety of events such as a Belgian market, concerts, mummers' plays and there were also a Chinese illusionist, a palmist and lightning artist portraits.

A committee was set up in 1916 to organise the month-long exhibition 'Ancient and Modern Embroidery and Needlework', with various co-opted members, such as Phoebe Traquair, May Morris and the architect Sir Robert Lorimer. Items were borrowed from the Victoria and Albert Museum, London; Royal Scottish Museum, Edinburgh (now National Museums of Scotland); Bowes Museum, Barnard Castle; and from many private individuals including Princess Louise, Duchess of Argyll, and the distinguished

'Exhibition of Ancient and Modern Embroidery and Needlework', 1916

Banner designed and worked by Jessie Newbery and Ann Macbeth, 1901. Hessian and appliqué linen embroidered with gold metal threads and floss silk. Ann Macbeth stitched the City Arms, Jessie Newbery the other side.
Exhibited 1916, Glasgow School of Art.
Collection: British Association for the Advancement of Science. Photo Glasgow Museums

local collectors William Burrell and John A. Holms. Work by both Ann Macbeth and Jessie Newbery was included and Mrs Newbery also loaned various items including examples of peasant embroidery from Greece and Hungary. European peasant art provided an alternative aesthetic for artists of the Arts and Crafts Movement, an interest that flourished from the 1860s until the 1930s. These items would have been of particular fascination to the embroidery students. Macbeth and Newbery organised the display of more than one thousand items, which they arranged into three sections: Domestic, Military and Ecclesiastical.

A catalogue was produced which included an essay on Ayrshire whitework embroidery by James A. Morris, ARSA FRIBA, of which there were many fine examples in the exhibition. This industry, begun in the early 19th century, collapsed in the 1860s as a combined result of the American Civil War which restricted cotton imports and competition from cheaper machine-made embroidery from Switzerland. Ayrshire work is exquisite high-quality embroidery that depended on an extensive network of highly skilled outworkers throughout the west of Scotland and Ireland. They produced cuffs and collars but the finest work was usually reserved for baby robes and caps (figs 18 and 19). Several items from the exhibition have since been given to the School including a rare dated whitework sampler illustrating different lace filling stitches (fig. 17) and Jessie Newbery's mantel border (fig. 23) and cushion cover (fig. 24).

The Needlework Development Scheme, 1934-1962

The Needlework Development Scheme was set up and funded anonymously by J. & P. Coats' Central Agency in Glasgow in conjunction with the four Scottish Arts Schools: Aberdeen, Dundee, Edinburgh and Glasgow. The stated aim — to encourage greater interest in embroidery and raise the standard of design — was to be achieved through the setting-up of a design reference collection of historical and contemporary embroidery that would be available for study, and through attendant publications, lectures and exhibitions.

J. & P. Coats, thread manufacturers of Paisley, were a major British Company trading internationally with mills in Russia, Poland, Germany, Austria, Spain, Portugal, Belgium, Italy, Switzerland, Canada, Mexico and Japan, as well as forty associated and subsidiary companies. Their influence was considerable. They were market leaders who advertised widely, published their own booklets, placed articles in various journals such as *Stickereien und Spitzen* and financed *The Needlewoman* journal, published in London. They invested heavily in the Needlework Development Scheme and doubtless saw it as a way of increasing the market for their threads.

Anonymous funding enabled the scheme to involve publicly funded bodies such as educational authorities and museums, which would have been impossible had any commercial motivation been overt. Initially, the Principals of the four Schools were responsible for its organisation and the heads of the embroidery departments played an important role in selecting work, although undoubtedly Coats influenced the content of the collection.

Dorothy Angus at Aberdeen and Louisa Chart at Edinburgh were responsible for selecting modern British Embroidery; Kathleen Mann from Glasgow, Head of the Embroidery Department from 1931–34, visited France and Italy. The emphasis was on recent work and historical examples formed only 10% of the collection made during the 1930s, although many of these items are of the highest quality, such as the belt with purse and pincushion (fig. 2). Some of them were bought from dealers or donated by collectors such as John Jacoby. He kept the important Jacoby Ilke collection in Switzerland, but he gave the fragment of blackwork (fig. 1). He already knew Glasgow School of Art, having organised an exhibition of items from his collection and lectured there in 1936.

The best pieces of contemporary embroidery collected by the NDS during the 1930s were from other European countries which at the time were at the forefront of design. Coats had contacts which facilitated such acquisitions. But this appreciation of non-British textiles was not confined to Coats. There was an awareness of European and South Asian textiles among local people in the West of Scotland through trade in textiles and through Glasgow's international exhibitions. As a result of such an enlightened policy, GSA has an outstanding collection of European work, particularly from Germany and Austria (figs 55–57 and 60–64).

The preponderance of religious subjects was probably at the suggestion of Coats and Heffernan suggests that Glasgow's *Madonna and Two Angels* (fig. 57) and Dundee's *Madonna and Holy Family*, both by Emmy Zweybrück, are unlike any of the previous designs done before she began work for Coats in 1934. The items from Amsterdam are also of note. The item entitled *The Love of God for Man* is dated 1937 in the NDS inventory and is very probably the Grand Prix award-winning design Louisa Chart purchased when she visited the 1937 Paris Exhibition.

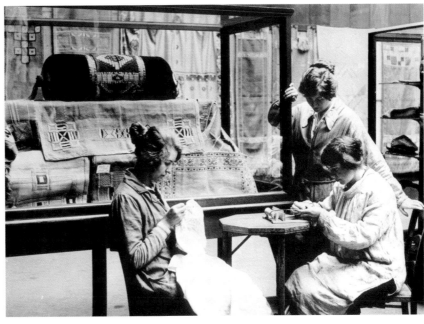

Students embroidering in the School's museum c1920s. On the left is the painter Mary Armour who became Honorary President of the School.

After the First World War, the main driving forces at the School had retired and design in Glasgow had lost momentum and in the rest of Britain had become entrenched in its own traditional styles. However, in London, Rebecca Crompton provided the impetus for a more modern dynamic, spontaneous expression in embroidery, more in keeping with design developments in the decorative and fine arts and architecture. One of her students, Kathleen Mann (1908–2000), was appointed to Glasgow in 1931 where she emphasised contemporary design and introduced new techniques such as machine embroidery which she used with flair and assurance. Examples of her work were included in the 'Modern Embroidery' exhibition held at the Victoria and Albert Museum in 1932, which also included work by Macbeth and Crompton, and by European artists such as Emmy Zweybrück (fig. 56). Crompton was invited to undertake the first lecture

'Little Visitor' by Kathleen Mann, mid 1930s, frontispiece of *Appliqué Design and Method*, 1937, one of a series of books written by Kathleen Mann. The panel worked in appliqué with hand and machine embroidery is in the collection of Glasgow Museums.

LIVERPOOL JOHN MOORES UNIVERSITY LEARNING SERVICES

Hanging: *The Love of God for Man*, 1937 F29 (NDS 514) Designed and worked by E.T. Hoost, Amsterdam. Embroidered in muted colours on natural linen in a wide variety of filling patterns. 58 × 39¾in. (147 × 99cm)

tour initiated in 1937 during which she visited the four Scottish Art Schools. In 1946, Madame Pavlu, an expert on Slovak Embroidery, came from Czechoslovakia and, in 1948, Mrs Gertie Wandel, President of the Haanarbejdts Fremme (the Danish Handcrafts Guild), Copenhagen, lectured at eight venues throughout the country.

Initially, the Scheme only involved Scotland and the intention was to form a design reference collection of British and foreign embroidery that would be available to schools, training colleges, women's institutes as well as the art schools. The Scheme was closed in 1939 with the outbreak of war when government restrictions were placed on imports and manufacturers forced to divert production to the war effort. By this time almost nine hundred embroideries had been collected.

In 1945 the Scheme was revived and extended to the rest of Britain. An Advisory Committee was formed, consisting of a representative from the Ministry of Education, the Scottish Education Department, the Victoria and Albert Museum and the NDS Glasgow. In addition it was decided to appoint an embroidery expert for a two-year term; the first, Kay Köhler, was appointed in 1946. She was succeeded in 1948 by Ulla Kockum from Stockholm, formerly a designer for embroidery and weaving at Jönköping Läns Hemslojdsforening, Sweden. The purpose of frequent changes was to maintain a lively fresh approach and to ensure contact with a wide range of designers.

Publications were an important part of the Scheme. Two bulletins, *And So to Sew* (1949–58) and *And So to Embroider* (1949–58), were published three times a year and were free until 1958 when demand reached such a peak that a small charge was made for multiple copies of a single issue. Each bulletin or leaflet contained information on a technique, together with a suitable design project that was clearly illustrated and explained. The first booklet *Contemporary Embroideries. The Needlework Development Scheme in Scotland, Illustrating some of the Works Belonging to the Collection Acquired by the Four Central Art Institutions in Scotland, under a Scheme for the Development of Needlework in Scotland* was published in 1938, of which the frontispiece is *Pietà*, 1934 (fig. 60). Subsequently a wide range of publications was issued, ranging from *And So to Begin* (1953) for use in primary schools to *Decorative Stitching with the Sewing Machine* (1956), *Designing from Traditional Embroideries* (1959) and, in 1952, Ulla Kockum (as Ulla Kockum-Øverengen) wrote *Embroideries of Sweden* (*see* Bibliography).

Ulla Kockum and Kathleen Whyte became great friends. Kath Whyte took over as Head of Embroidery and Woven Textiles at GSA in 1948. She made effective use of the NDS collection in her teaching and the influence of the embroidery from Münster (figs 62, 62a and 63) can be seen in both choice of subject matter and treatment for some of her own and her students' work during the late 1950s. For example, her piece entitled *The Last Supper* in the National Museums of Scotland and Veronica Togneri's *Creation* in Glasgow Museums both have an expressive simplicity of design.

Weaving was introduced by Agnes McCredie (Head of Department, 1934–48), who succeeded Kathleen Mann (Head of Department, 1931–34). Kath Whyte had studied weaving with Ethel Mairet at Ditchling and was to become an inspiring teacher of both disciplines. With widespread interest in Scandinavian design, after the war she travelled to Sweden to visit weaving centres such as Gothenburg and Boros, as well as Stockholm. She was impressed by Sweden where craft design had evolved successfully and adapted to modern life, which was an issue of concern in Britain, as it lagged behind other European countries. The belief that traditional crafts should take account of modern design ideas was also one of the motivating factors for the NDS.

In the post-war years there was a dynamic atmosphere at GSA. The Departments of Embroidery and Weaving, of Printed Textiles, of Graphics, of Silversmithing and of Interior Design (that constituted the Design School) were housed together in a sepa-

Needlework Development Scheme leaflets

Diploma Show, 1953

Student working in the Embroidery and Woven Textile Department, late 1960s

rate building and enjoyed camaraderie and close interaction. This is evident in the collaborative work of Kath Whyte and Robert Stewart, Head of Printed Textiles (figs 40 & 41).

Inevitably, particularly close links between the School and Coats would develop as they were situated quite close to each other in the centre of Glasgow. Some GSA students went on to work for Coats in the 1950s but one Hannah Frew left Coats to become a student at Glasgow School of Art and eventually became Kath Whyte's assistant. The Needlework Development Scheme headquarters was also a useful resource for students and staff as there was a study room of the specimens not in circulation, a photographic and record index of the collection and a library of reference books available to visitors.

In 1961 the Scheme was brought to a close, as it was believed that it had achieved its aims, by which time over five thousand items had been acquired. The collection and records were dispersed to various organisations interested in embroidery throughout the country. These included various bodies such as the Federation of Women's Institutes, National Union of Townswomen's Guilds, various museums and museum educational services, and Colleges of Education. The largest number went to the Embroiderers' Guild and many of the most important items to the Victoria and Albert Museum and the Royal Scottish Museum, Edinburgh (National Museums of Scotland). Each of the four Scottish Art Schools received a minimum of one hundred pieces. GSA received one hundred and twenty-five items, the largest single component of the textile archive. Of these, seventy-one are British and fifty-four foreign. It is possible that there were other items, too, now lost.

Recent Years

The NDS gift remained the main study collection within the Embroidery and Woven Textiles Department for many years but additional items such as the Donald Brothers weave sample books and weave catalogues and samples from Bute Fabrics have been added. With the amalgamation in 1999 of the two textile departments into a single Textile Department combining embroidery, weaving, knitting and printed textiles and the increasing emphasis on individual research, the textile archive has assumed greater importance. Textiles which had been kept in different School buildings were brought together with the School's documentary archive in a single Study Centre. This facilitates research of this valuable resource. Inevitably there are gaps in the collection but it is hoped that through judicious accessions to develop the archive and reflect the work of the School, the Study Centre will provide students with both a sense of history and inspiration for their own creative work.

Recently additions have been mainly by individual gifts. For example, after Kath Whyte's death in 1996, her executors gave a quantity of her drawings, designs, samples and correspondence to the School, among them *Stitch Tree* (fig. 48). As a direct result of Sandra Heffernan's research, the original design for *Hebridean Village* (fig. 38) was donated.

The most significant development in making the collection more widely accessible has been the Scottish Textile Heritage Online project, led by Heriot Watt University and funded by the Scottish Museums Council. This project surveyed and documented textile collections in six Scottish museums and archives, including Glasgow School of Art, that can be accessed on www.scottishtextiles.org.uk. Further information about GSA's archive can be obtained on the School's website: www.archives@gsa.ac.uk. The collection is available by appointment with the archivist, tel: +44 (0) 141 353 4592.

Notes

1 *Transactions of the National Association for the Advancement of Art and its Application to Industry*, Edinburgh Meeting, 1889, London, 1890
2 Gleeson White, 'Some Glasgow Designers and Their Work', *The Studio*, 1898, vol. 12, p. 48 and p. 51
3 Review notice, *The Studio*, vol. 26, 1902, p. 101
4 J. Taylor, 'Modern Decorative Art at Glasgow', *The Studio*, vol. 39, 1906, p. 31
5 Mary Sturrock in conversation with the author, 1989
6 GSA Annual Report, 1914–15
7 *The Daily Province*, Vancouver, 9 September 1922
8 GSA Annual Reports for the years 1914–17

Selection of Items from the Textile Archive

Fig. 7a

Sizes are given in inches and (centimetres)
Height precedes width

Abbreviations: GSA Glasgow School of Art
      NDS Needlework Development Scheme
      NDSS Needlework Development Scheme in Scotland

GSA accession references (against each caption title and elsewhere) come in
various forms and should be used for access to archive material.

BRITISH

Embroidery

Fig. 1 Flower motif, late 16th century

GB1 (NDS 1367)

A formal motif representing a sprig of honeysuckle worked in black silk on linen in geometric patterns in Holbein stitch, outlined in chain stitch in silver-gilt thread. Much of the outline is restoration and the motif has been mounted on modern linen. This work may have been carried out in Coats studio. 5¼ × 4¼in. (13 × 11cm) Blackwork embroidery rarely survives in good condition because the logwood dye used rots the silk thread.

Another identical motif and two related carnation motifs, donated to the Needlework Development Scheme by John Jacoby, are in the Embroiderers' Guild Collection (EG 206). They probably originally formed part of a cover for a long cushion which may have been cut up when worn or to re-use the embroidery in a new design. This was common practice in the 16th and 17th centuries. Designs for household furnishings would be drawn professionally or copied from pattern books or herbals with commonly grown flowers and fruit the most popular subjects. They often have symbolic meaning e.g. honeysuckle represented affection and fidelity.

LITERATURE

Sandra Heffernan, PhD Thesis, *Design from Artefacts: Innovate or Imitate: Issues of Aesthetics, Education, Collecting, Making and Marketing in Coats' Needlework Development Scheme: 1934–1962*

Pauline Johnson, *Three Hundred Years of Embroidery 1600–1900, Treasures from the Embroiderers' Guild of Great Britain*, 1987, p. 25

J. L. Nevinson, 'Needlework in the Home in the Times of Queen Elizabeth and James I', *Embroidery*, September 1936, pp 80–81

Figs 2 & 2a (detail) Belt with purse and pincushion, early 17th century

GB2 (NDS 3932)

Plaited silk belt with silver fastenings from which are suspended, on plaited silk cords, a tapestry woven silk and metal thread purse and pincushion. The purse has a floral design and is decorated at the corners with metal threads in the form of crowns. It has a drawstring fastening with two wooden-cored tassels. The pincushion has a bird design. The fine weave has 24 warps to the inch (2.5cm). Belt is 27in. (68.5cm) long, the purse is 5in. (12.5cm) square, the pincushion 2½in. (6.5cm) square. The making of cords and tassels was highly skilled and books of instruction were published.

Pincushions were important as pins were a necessity to hold different pieces of clothing, such as sleeves and bodices, together when worn. Pincushions sometimes appear in portraits together with other status symbols such as caskets of jewellery, because pins were expensive. A man could only make twenty in a day and it is possible that the term 'pin money' derives from the need for women to save up to buy them.

Fig. 3 Whitework sampler, mid 17th century

GB3 (NDS 100)

Linen with linen thread in cut and drawn work with needlepoint fillings. The figures on the bottom row include a mermaid and woman and child. 19 × 6¾in. (48.5 × 17cm)

From a simple band sampler girls progressed to more complex and technically demanding cut-work samplers made with white linen threads on white linen. Patterns were built up, using buttonhole stitches, on a framework of diagonal threads laid down after the squares of fabric had been cut away. Some of the earliest embroidery pattern books contain designs for cut-work. Among the most popular was Richard Schorleyker's *A Schole-house for the Needle* published in 1624. On the title page he claimed: 'Here followeth certaine patterns of cut-workes newly invented and never published before'. There was obviously a demand for such a book as it ran to twelve editions.

Figs 4 & 4a (detail) Embroidered picture, dated 1652

GB4 (NDS 4105)

Silk satin embroidered with silk threads and decorated with coral, garnet beads, pearls and mother of pearl shell, the windows are of mica. The flower petals and clothes are worked in detached buttonhole stitch, the monogram M C and date, at man's feet, are in seed pearls. 10 × 15in. (25.5 × 38cm)

Raised work pictures of a man and woman standing in a pleasure garden surrounded by a random arrangement of birds, fruit and flowers became popular during the third quarter of the 17th century. They may represent an engagement or marriage with the couple shown in an Arcadian garden of love. But secular and religious meanings overlap as the garden of love is also linked to the religious idea of Paradise.

LITERATURE
Needlework Development Scheme, A *Review of the Aims and Activities of the Needlework Development Scheme*, Needlework Development Scheme, Glasgow, 1960

Figs 5 & 5a (detail) Sampler, signed AB or RB 1669

GB5 (NDS 899)

Linen with silk threads in a design of alphabets, geometric patterns and flower motifs in a wide variety of stitches. 35 × 6¾in. (89 × 17cm)

Long narrow samplers with horizontal bands of patterns were a child's first exercise once they had mastered the rudiments of needlework. The sampler became a record of stitches and patterns that would be required to mark and decorate household and personal linen and consequently was kept rolled up in a workbox for reference.

Fig. 6 Chair seat, Scottish, late 17th or early 18th century
GB6 (NDS 515)
Chain stitch in wool on linen. 15¼ × 19½in. (39 × 49.5cm)

Figs 7 & 7a (detail – see page 18) Embroidered and quilted bedcover, early 18th century
GB12 (NDS 1058)
The central panel is of linen embroidered with exotic flower and bird motifs in fine wool chain stitch, probably tamboured. A border has been added and the whole quilted in an elaborate design. The embroidery is probably Indian from Gujarat (for the European market), which has been made up and quilted in Britain. 91 × 96½in. (232 × 246cm)

Tambour is a type of chain stitch embroidery worked with a fine hook. Initially a technique used in India it is a quick method of achieving a continuous line of stitching. Tambouring became a fashionable pursuit for European women in the 1770s and from the late 18th to the mid 19th century white muslin dresses and accessories were frequently decorated with this work (see fig. 15).

There is another similar bedspread of this date made from tamboured fragments in the collection. (MCT 1004)

Fig. 8 Fragment of embroidery, early 18th century
GB9 (NDS 3933)
Silk thread in chain stitch and French knots on linen. The background is worked in back stitch to resemble quilting. 9¼ × 13 in. (23.5 × 33cm)

Fig. 9 Baby's shirt, 18th century
GB11 (NDS 1391)
White lawn with hollie point insertions on the shoulder incorporating the initials A.M. The hem is finished with drawn threadwork and an embroidered edge. 10¾in. (27.5cm) long

Hollie point is a British lace worked in small buttonhole stitches. It is mainly found on the shoulders of baby shirts and the crown of baby caps dating from the 18th century although it was in use during the 16th and 17th centuries when it was also used to decorated household linen.

Fig. 10 Part of an apron, early 18th century
GB8 (NDS 4106)
Scallop-edged silk taffeta embroidered with silk and metal threads, pearls and sequins. The floral design has areas of metal thread embroidery padded with cord.
16 × 37½in. (40.5 × 95cm)

LITERATURE
Needlework Development Scheme, *A Review of the Aims and Activities of the Needlework Development Scheme*, Needlework Development Scheme, Glasgow, 1960

Fig. 11 **Man's waistcoat, late 18th century**

GB15 (NDS 124)

Corded silk embroidered with silk threads. The floral design includes roses, thistles and shamrocks. 23in. (58.5cm) long

Fig. 12 **Man's waistcoat, late 18th century**

GB16 (NDS 1311)

Floral design worked in silk thread in satin stitch on satin and with embroidered buttons. 25½in. (65cm) long

Fig. 13 **Fragment of a border, early 19th century**

GB23 (NDS 1547)

Black silk embroidery on white cotton in buttonhole and running stitches.
5 × 16in. (12.5 × 41cm)

Fig. 14 **Corner of a handkerchief, early 19th century**

GB27 (NDS 1707)

White muslin with whitework embroidery and lace filling stitches. The initials may have been added later. 9 × 9½in. (23 × 24cm)

Fig. 15 **Woman's apron c1820s**

GB20

Muslin tamboured with a floral design in woollen yarn. 25½in. (65cm) long 49½in. (125cm) wide at hem

Fig. 16 **Panel for a pole screen, c1830**

GB25 (NDS 5264)

Posy of flowers worked in silk threads on a silk ground in stem stitch. The naturalistic flowers are bluebell, rose, lilies, pansies and daffodil. 11½ × 10 in. (29 × 25.5cm)

Fig. 17 **Samples of lace filling stitches, signed: E McG 1837**

GB26

Worked by E. McGaan, Ayrshire. 8 × 9in. (20.2 × 22.8cm)

Lace filling stitches are an important identifying characteristic of Ayrshire whitework.

EXHIBITED
1916   Glasgow – 'Ancient and Modern Embroidery and Needlecraft' (418),
Glasgow School of Art
Gift of Miss Tolmie, Glasgow

Figs 18, 18a & 18b (detail) **Baby robe, Ayrshire work, mid 19th century**
GB28
Muslin embroidered with white cotton thread in satin stitch with a variety of lace filling stitches. Length 48in. (122cm)

The embroidery was also known as flowered muslin and produced from the early 19th century until the mid 1860s. The designs, together with the number of hours allowed for the work, were printed on muslin then taken to outworkers throughout the west of Scotland and Northern Ireland by an agent. Solid satin stitch outlines were worked before the fabric was cut away and filled with needlepoint lace stitches. The embroidery was also used to decorate collars, cuffs, caps and other small items that were exported world-wide. The major Glasgow companies exhibited at the '1851 International Exhibition', Crystal Palace, London, causing one reviewer to comment: 'A large proportion of the articles exhibited are for those small specimens of humanity upon whom mothers are frequently inclined to lavish very large sums and in truth, the robes, caps and especially the quilt, form a tempting display.'

Fig. 19 **Baby's bonnet, Ayrshire work c1862**
GB32 (NDS 1276)
Made for the children of G. D. Fullerton
The crowns could be bought separately, ready worked for making up or replacing worn and damaged embroidery.

Figs 20 & 20a **Two designs for block printed shawls 1840s–50s**
DC39
Hand drawn and painted in gouache on card. 21 × 15¾in. (84 × 40cm), 25 × 15¼in. (63.5 × 38.5cm)

From a collection of 26 boards of designs for Paisley shawls bought by T. C. Campbell Mackie, lecturer at the School from 1921 to 50, Head of the Design and Craft Department 1932–45.
Gift of T. C. Campbell, 1949

Fig. 21 **Tea cosy made by Miss Robertson, Glasgow, 1880s**
GSAT 103
Velvet with appliqué embroidered with silk and metal threads in feather, blanket and straight stitches with beads. Padded and lined with purple silk. 9¼ × 13in. (23.5 × 32cm)

During the 1880s there was a vogue for crazy patchwork, also known as Kaleidoscope, puzzle or Japanese patchwork. Haphazardly arranged fabrics, most usually silks and velvets, were often overlapped and joined with feather stitch in contrasting threads. The patchwork was further embellished with stars, butterflies and spiders webs worked in beads, sequins and threads.

Fig. 22 Banner designed by Walter Crane, worked by his wife Mary Frances Crane, 1893

GSAT 437

The design drawn in pencil on linen ground (faded) is worked with silk, wool, cotton and gold thread in long and short, satin, running stitches and couching. 65½ × 34in. (166 × 87cm)

The motto 'Qui Corvus Pascit Pascere Potest Grues' meaning 'he who feeds the raven is able to feed the crane'. The arms are those of Sir Francis Crane, tapestry weaver to King Charles I at the Mortlake workshops and were used by Walter's father Thomas Crane, who was believed to be a descendant.

Walter Crane (1845–1915) is best known as an illustrator, particularly of children's books, and industrial designer especially of wallpapers. He was a member of the Arts and Crafts Exhibition Society and concerned with art education. Among his many designs for embroidered banners were large elaborate figure panels representing Music, Painting, Architecture and Poetry for the 'Philadelphia Centennial Exhibition', 1876. They hung in the successful Royal School of Needlework pavilion that stimulated interest in art needlework in America and that resulted in the setting-up of branches of the Royal School of Needlework in Philadelphia and Boston.
Purchased by GSA at the sale of his studio's contents in 1922–3

Fig. 23 Mantel border, designed by Jessie Newbery, worked by her aunt, Edith Rowat, mid 1890s

GB43 (GSAT 441)

Natural linen with a border of drawn threadwork, embroidered with crewel wool in long and short, satin, stem straight stitches and French knots. 26 × 99½in. (66 × 252.7cm)

EXHIBITED
1896 London – Fifth Gallery, Regent Street (242)
1916 Glasgow – 'Ancient and Modern Embroidery and Needlecraft', Glasgow School of Art
1980 Glasgow – 'Glasgow School of Art Embroidery 1894–1920' (109), Art Gallery and Museum, Kelvingrove

LITERATURE
The Studio, vol. 12, 1897, p. 48
The largest collection of her work is held by Glasgow Museums.

Fig. 24 Cushion cover designed by Jessie Newbery, worked by Edith Rowat, 1890s

GB42 (GSAT 440)

Unbleached linen embroidered with crewel wool in stem, straight, running and satin stitches with French knots. 27½ × 27½in. (71 × 71cm)

EXHIBITED
1916 Glasgow – 'Ancient and Modern Embroidery and Needlecraft', Glasgow
1980 Glasgow – 'Glasgow School of Art Embroidery 1894–1920' (95), Art Gallery and Museum, Kelvingrove

Fig. 25 Design for a pulpit fall, Jessie R. Newbery c1899

NMC 006

Pencil and watercolour. Inscription: Be ye doers of the word and not hearers only.

14 × 19¾in. (35.5 × 50.1cm)

EXHIBITED

1899 London – 'Arts and Crafts Exhibition' (possibly 629)

1971 Glasgow – 'Fra H. Newbery' (18), Glasgow School of Art

1980 Glasgow – 'Glasgow School of Art Embroidery 1894–1920' (112), Art Gallery and Museum, Kelvingrove

1988 Glasgow – 'Glasgow Girls', Glasgow School of Art

1990 Glasgow – 'Glasgow Girls: Women in Art & Design 1880–1920' (34), Art Gallery and Museum, Kelvingrove

1992 London and tour – 'Out of the Frame', Crafts Council

LITERATURE

Burkhauser, Jude (editor), *Glasgow Girls: Women in Art and Design 1880–1920*, Canongate, 1990, p. 23

Fig. 26 Banner designed by Ann Macbeth, early 1900s

GSAT 417

Coarse canvas with linen appliqué, embroidered with wool and silver gilt threads, glass beads and buttons. The stylised arms are those of the city of Glasgow with its patron Saint Mungo.

25½ × 92½in. (65 × 235cm)

Fig. 27 Triptych, signed and dated: MHP 1903 AD

GSAT 415

Worked by Maggie Hamilton Paterson in silks, gold and silver thread with beads.

A note on the back states 'started 1901 completed 1903'. Centre panel 40½ × 24½in. (103 × 61.6cm) side panels 35¾ × 15¾in. (91 × 31cm). In an elaborate contemporary frame 55¼ × 72¾in. (140 × 185cm)

Maggie Hamilton was the wife of the architect A. N. Paterson, brother of the artist James Paterson, one of the Glasgow Boys. Although an amateur needlewoman with no formal training she frequently exhibited large intensively worked embroideries. Other works by Maggie Hamilton are in the collection of the National Museum of Scotland and Glasgow Museum.

EXHIBITED

1911 Glasgow – 'Scottish National Exhibition of History and Industry'

1916 Glasgow – 'Ancient and Modern Embroidery and Needlecraft' (765), Glasgow School of Art

1977 London – 'The Paterson Family 1877–1977', Belgrave Gallery

Gift of Colonel Paterson, Helensburgh

Fig. 28 Pair of panels, designed and worked by Margaret Macdonald Mackintosh, c1904–8

MC A1a&b

Linen embroidered with silk and metal threads in satin stitch and couching with silk braid, ribbons, silk appliqué, glass beads, square linen buttons painted gold. The faces are painted in watercolour on white kid stretched over card. 71¾ × 16in. (182.2 × 40.6cm)

Commissioned by Mr and Mrs Walter Blackie for the bedroom of the Hill House, Helensburgh. Anne Ellis's research has shown that the Blackie family were on holiday near Turin in 1902 and as Mrs Blackie's sister Jane Younger and Charles Rennie Mackintosh, who designed the Hill House, were exhibiting at the 'Turin International Exhibition of Decorative Art' they may well have visited it. In the Scottish Section they would have seen attenuated figure panels by Margaret Macdonald for the Rose Boudoir which may have led to this commission. Similar panels had also been incorporated into Mackintosh's room scheme exhibited at the eighth exhibition of the Vienna Secession in 1900. The panels remained at Hill House until 1953 when they were removed and given to Glasgow School of Art.

EXHIBITED
1933 Glasgow – 'Charles Rennie Mackintosh Memorial Exhibition' (134, 157), McLellan Galleries
1961 Turin – 'Figure di un Epoca', Mostra della Mode
1968 Edinburgh and London – 'Charles Rennie Mackintosh Centenary' (236), Royal Scottish Museum and Victoria and Albert Museum
1973 Milan – 'La Sedie di Charles Rennie Mackintosh', Triennale di Milano
1977 Helensburgh – Royal Institute of Architects in Scotland, Hill House
1980 Glasgow – 'Glasgow School of Art Embroidery 1894–1920' (68), Art Gallery and Museum, Kelvingrove
1983 Edinburgh – '1900 Vienna Secession reconstruction', Fine Art Society
1983 Glasgow – 'Margaret Macdonald Mackintosh', Hunterian Art Gallery
1988 London – 'Japan & Britain: an aesthetic dialogue', Barbican Art Gallery
1988 Italy – 'Charles Rennie Mackintosh', Certaldo
1990 Glasgow – 'Glasgow Girls', Art Gallery and Museum, Kelvingrove
1992 London, – 'Arts & Crafts to Avant Garde', South Bank Centre
2000 London and Tokyo – 'Art Nouveau', Victoria and Albert Museum

LITERATURE
Burkhauser, Jude (editor), *Glasgow Girls: Women in Art and Design 1880–1920*, Canongate, 1990, p. 83
Gift of W. G. Blackie, 1953

Fig. 29 Bible markers, possibly designed and worked by Ann Macbeth, c1908–14

GSAT 421

Corded silk embroidered with silk threads in satin, back stitch and couched gold thread and a ribbon fringe with glass beads (some missing). 2¼ × 54½in. (6 × 138cm) excluding 1in. (2.5cm) fringe

Gift of Margaret Walker

Fig. 30 Dress designed and made by Daisy McGlashan, c1910

GSAT 472

Green silk with violet velvet appliqué and white silk thread in satin stitch. The colours chosen were those of the women's suffrage movement, representing the slogan 'give women votes'. Original photograph shows McGlashan wearing the dress.

EXHIBITED

1988 Glasgow – 'Glasgow Girls', Glasgow School of Art
1990 Glasgow – 'Glasgow Girls: Women in Art & Design 1880–1920' (28), 1990, Art Gallery and Museum, Kelvingrove
1992–3 London and tour – 'Out of the Frame', Crafts Council
1999 Japan – 'Liberty Style' (123), 1999
2004 USA – 'The Arts and Crafts of Europe and America 1880–1920: Design for the Modern World', Los Angeles County Museum

LITERATURE

Burkhauser, Jude (editor), *Glasgow Girls: Women in Art and Design 1880–1920*, Canongate, 1990, p. 53
Gift of her daughters Daisy Anderson and Violet Neish, 1984

Fig. 31 Collar designed and worked by Grace Melvin, c1912

Acc. 132

Black velvet trimmed with rabbit fur. Embroidered with two thicknesses of silk thread in satin stitch, needleweaving, darning and couching, with semi-circular and tulip shaped glass beads. Length 29in. (73.5cm). Neck edge to hem 11in. (25.4cm)

EXHIBITED

1980 'Glasgow School of Art Embroidery 1894–1920' (76), Art Gallery and Museum, Kelvingrove

Figs 32 & 32a (detail) Panel: *Carnival*, designed and worked by Molly Booker, signed and dated 1932

GB50 (NDS 301)

Linen canvas with wools, predominantly in long and short stitch with additional glass and metal beads, pearls, lace and feathers. 58 × 78in. (147.3 × 198cm)

Aileen Molly Booker trained at the Central School of Art and Craft, London. She worked on hessian in vividly coloured wools, mainly in stem and chain stitch. Her work was considered innovative in terms of design, technique and colour and an exhibition of her work was held at the Lefevre Gallery, London. In 1935 she wrote on embroidery design for a special number of *The Studio*.

LITERATURE

NDS, *Contemporary Embroideries*, 1938, illus. no. 43 (*see* Bibliography)

Fig. 33 Map: Midhurst the town in the midst of the woods, mid 1930s
GB53 (NDS 796)

Haslemere on the north, Chichester on the south, with roads, buildings and trees. Fine filoselle on cotton in tiny stem, chain and fly stitches. 15 × 13in. (38 × 33cm)

Fig. 34 Handkerchief sachet designed by Rebecca Crompton, 1938
GB57 (NDS 407)

Possibly worked by Dorothy Benson. Machine embroidery in silk on white silk ground. The design is of cupid dancing through flowers and leaves. 7¾ × 8in. (17 × 18cm)

Rebecca Crompton (1895–1947) trained at Derby School of Art and from 1923 taught at Croydon School of Art where she became a considerable force through her innovative approach to embroidery. She wrote *Modern Design in Embroidery* (1936) in which she encouraged vitality, spontaneity, experimentation and self-expression in design. She also encouraged the combination of different techniques including the use of machine embroidery. As part of the Needlework Development Scheme's promotion in 1937 Crompton undertook a successful lecture tour of Scottish art schools. Other examples of her work are held in the collections of the National Museums of Scotland, Victoria and Albert Museum and Pickford House Museum, Derby.

Fig. 35 Teacosy designed by Rebecca Crompton 1938
GB56 (NDS 416)

Possibly worked by Dorothy Benson. Machine embroidered in cotton thread on silk , with a quilted lining. 10½ × 13¾in. 26.5 × 35cm

Benson worked in the embroidery department of Singer from 1916 until 1962 including the education section where teachers were trained in the use of the domestic machine. Among them was Rebecca Crompton and later Benson frequently demonstrated at Crompton's lectures.

LITERATURE
The Essential Guide to Embroidery, Murdoch Books, 2002, p. 215

Fig. 36 Missal cover designed and worked by Joan Mary Nicholson, 1950
GB61 (NDS 2910)

Satin with coloured silk in split stitch and couching. 6½ × 3½in. (16.5 × 9cm)

Joan Nicholson (b.1924) trained at West Hartlepool College of Art and the Royal College of Art before teaching at Farnham College of Art. She was a member of the Society of Industrial Artists receiving many commissions including for the Festival of Britain and the Royal Yacht Britannia.

Figs 37 & 37a (detail) **Nursery tablecloth: Weather House, 1947**

GB59 (NDS 1351)

Designed by Frances Beal, worked entirely on a domestic sewing machine by Dorothy Benson. 41 in. square (104cm)

Benson's consummate skill was highly regarded. She demonstrated that the domestic machine could imitate 47 stitches and methods of embroidery without the use of special attachments. She was frequently asked to work designs by other textile artists.

LITERATURE

Needlework Development Scheme, *A Review of the Aims and Activities of the Needlework Development Scheme*, Needlework Development Scheme, Glasgow, 1960, p. 16

Fig. 38 Panel: Hebridean Village c1950

A2 (NDS 4799)

Designed by Scottish artist Eric Loundsbach, worked by primary and secondary school children. Linen with appliqué in felt, linen, net, chenille with wool embroidery and a fringe. 16½ × 56¼in. (42 × 143cm)

LITERATURE

Buildings in Embroidery, And So To Embroider, NDS Bulletin 34
The original design for this work has recently been given to the archive by Elizabeth Geddes.

Fig. 39 Experimental panel, designed and machine embroidered by Robert Stewart, 1950

GB63 (NDS 2955)

Folder of three panels: left, three figures, 5in. (12.7cm) square; centre, signed 'Stewart' (shown) is 9½ × 5in. (24 × 12.7cm), right, entitled 'Taurus' is 5½ × 3¾in. (14 × 9.5cm)

EXHIBITED

2003 Glasgow and London – 'Robert Stewart, Design 1946–95', Glasgow School of Art and Goldsmith's College

LITERATURE

Liz Arthur, *Robert Stewart, Design 1946–95*, London, 2003, p. 34
Liz Arthur, *Kathleen Whyte Embroiderer*, Batsford, 1989, p. 46

Fig. 40 Design for embroidery by Robert Stewart, 1950

Acc. 37

Gouache, ink and gold paint on paper. 6½ × 4½in. (16.5 × 11.5cm)

LITERATURE

Liz Arthur, *Kathleen Whyte Embroiderer*, London, 1989, p 47

Liz Arthur, *Robert Stewart Design 1946–95*, London, 2003, p. 34

An interpretation of this design was worked by Kathleen Whyte and the works exchanged. Stewart kept the embroidery and Whyte the design. The embroidered panel has since been lost.

Figs 41 & 41a (detail of the back of the cushion) Cushion cover designed by Robert Stewart, worked by Kathleen Whyte, 1951

GB63 (NDS 2939)

Linen with cotton threads in a wide variety of stitches. 19 × 21in. (48 × 53.5cm)

Commissioned by the NDS for their Festival of Britain touring exhibition. Robert Stewart was Head of Printed Textiles 1949–84 and Kathleen Whyte Head of Embroidery and Weaving 1948–74 at GSA. They collaborated on three works, another cushion commissioned by the NDS is in the National Museum of Scotland.

EXHIBITED

1951 tour to ten towns – Needlework Development Scheme's 'Festival of Britain'
2003 Glasgow and London – 'Robert Stewart, Design 1946–95', Glasgow School of Art and Goldsmith's College

LITERATURE

Liz Arthur, *Robert Stewart, Design 1946–95*, London, 2003, p. 35

Fig. 42 Doll representing the novelist Walter Scott, c1956

DC38

Designed and made by Anne Scott. 11¾in. (30cm) high

A graduate of Edinburgh College of Art, Scott was commissioned by Sir Harry Jefferson Barnes when he was Glasgow School of Art's Deputy Director, to produce a series of British historical figures. It is not known how many there were in the original series, as some have subsequently been damaged beyond repair; however, twenty-seven survive in the collection.

Fig. 43 Dolls representing the painter Allan Ramsay (1713–84) and his second wife Margaret Lindsay, c1956

DC38

Designed and made by Anne Scott, 11¾in. (30cm) high

Margaret Lindsay's clothes are based on the portrait by her husband, c1758–60, in the National Gallery of Scotland.

Fig. 44 Sampler designed by Geraldine White, worked by Beryl Dean, 1958

GB68 (NDS 5056)

Three interpretations of a steeple design in different types of metal thread used in different techniques. Each 7¼ × 2in. (18.5 × 5cm)

Beryl Dean (1911–2001) trained at the Royal School of Needlework, the Bromley College of Art and the Royal College of Art and is renowned for pioneering a bold modern style of ecclesiastical embroidery. Her commissions include those for St Paul's London, Canterbury, Chelmsford, Guildford and Hereford Cathedrals, the Royal Chapel, Windsor Castle, and a frontal for St Giles Church, Northbrook, Illinois, USA. She was awarded the MBE in 1975.

Fig. 45 Decorative animal made by Shirley Tweedale, Rochdale Grammar School, Greater Manchester, 1959

GB70 (NDS 5165)

Felt, beads and metal threads. 5in. (12.7cm) high. Bulls were a popular motif during the 1950s, frequently appearing on ceramics and graphics.

LITERATURE
A similar one is illustrated in Mary Eirewen Jones' *A History of Western Embroidery*, London, Studio Vista, 1969

Fig. 46 Tablecloth designed and worked by Pat Miller, 1960

GB71 (NDS 5277)

Linen with cotton threads in a wide variety of stitches. A Grace 'God bless our food and make us good' is worked around the border. 34 × 33in. (86.5 × 84cm)

Fig. 47 *Apples*, designed and made by Mary Gribble, mid 1970s

DC29

Padded satin, leather and felt with couched metallic thread. 13¾ × 12¾in. (35 × 32.4cm)

LITERATURE
Hannah Frew, *Three-Dimensional Embroidery*, Van Nostrand Reinhold, 1975, pp 34–5

Fig. 48 Panel: *Stitch Tree*, designed and worked by Kathleen Whyte, 1977

DC29

Woollen ground with wools and silks in straight and rosette chain stitches. 18½ × 16in. (47 × 40.5cm) Kathleen Whyte (1909–96) was fascinated by her visual disturbance following a cataract operation. In this freely worked panel she explored the effect of light seen through a tree in her garden and attempts to capture the spontaneity of her initial rapid sketch.

Several major works by Kath Whyte are in the collection of Glasgow Museums, the National Museums of Scotland and many of her commissions can be found in Scottish churches. She was awarded the MBE in 1969 for services to Scottish Art Education.

LITERATURE
Liz Arthur, *Kathleen Whyte Embroiderer*, Batsford, 1989, pp 132–3

LIVERPOOL JOHN MOORES UNIVERSITY
LEARNING SERVICES

Fig. 49 **Panel designed and worked by Emma Robertson, 1985**

DC29

Random dyed silks and vilene with silk thread. Mounted on carved and painted board. 14½ × 9in. (36.2 × 24.5cm)

This student piece from Robertson's degree show was purchased by Kathleen Whyte.

Woven textiles

Fig. 50 **Sample Book, c1930s**

DC37/4/57

Jacquard woven linen created by N. & N. Lockhart & Sons Ltd for Donald Bros, Dundee. One of a collection of 67 sample books.

Donald Brothers Ltd (1896–1980) were linen canvas and furnishing fabric manufacturers. The company developed from the Dundee jute and linen industry, producing art fabrics that were used extensively in Arts and Crafts interiors and art galleries from 1896 until 1914. Between the 1930s and 1960s they gained international recognition for their high-quality linen furnishings, including prints and jacquard weaves marketed under the trade name Old Glamis Fabrics. Ann Macbeth designed for the company and, on one occasion, travelled to Austria with Mr Donald to investigate weave designs.

Knitted fabrics

Fig. 51 **Shetland shawl, c late 1870s**

EWT TC1/11

This shawl with traditional stitches and patterns was used for the donor's father Harold Borland, born in Glasgow in 1883, and for his older brother and sister. 44 × 91in. (111.7 × 231.2cm)

Knitting continues to flourish in Shetland and both boys and girls are still taught in Primary School.

Gift of Kristeen Holmes, daughter of Harold Borland

Fig. 52 **Knitting sampler, mid 19th century**

Acc. 133

Cotton knitted in the round in 15 different patterns for sock tops, said to have been knitted in India from a British pattern. 23in. (58.4cm) long

From the collection of Mary Medlam which was recently purchased from her by the Textile Department for use in the studio as a teaching aid.

Fig. 53 Doll's dress and baby cap, designed and worked by Mary Medlam, c1950–80s

Acc. 133

Muslin with knitted linen thread lace. Dress 11in. (28cm) long

From a large collection of samples and patterns by Mary Medlam who developed her own method of knitting lace. She used traditional patterns but also created her own designs and patterns. During the late 1940s and 1950s, she sold designs and samples to J. & P. Coats, sets of mats to Harrods, designs to *Pins and Needles*, Odhams periodicals (including *Woman*) and during the 1980s to Thorn Press.

Fig. 54 Two garments from a sample book of doll's clothes, designed and made by Mary Medlam, c1950–80s

Acc. 133

Knitted cotton. Each garment has its own set of instructions. 3½in. (9cm) and 4in. (10cm) long

EUROPEAN

Fig. 55 Circular table cover, Austrian or German, 1920s

F19

Darned net with stylised Art Deco figures in fashionable 1920s dress. 22in. (56cm) diameter

Fig. 56 Circular table cover Emmy Zweybrück-Prochaska, Austria, late 1920s

F20 (NDS)

Net embroidered with cotton in needle-run and darning stitches. 32¾in. (83cm) diameter

This design is the same as one exhibited at the 1932 'Modern Embroidery' exhibition at the Victoria and Albert Museum and similar to a set of designs done for the first-class saloon of the S. S. Bremen. The Bremen designs were worked at the Vereiunigte Werkstatten, Munich, where tapestries and embroideries were made for hotels, liners, airports, officers' quarters and the chancellery building in Berlin. (See Heffernan thesis)

LITERATURE

F. Brehaus de Groot, *Der Ozean Express Bremen*, Munich, 1930, pp 138 & 142
ed. C. Geoffrey Holme, *Modern Embroidery*, Special Spring Number of *The Studio*, 1933, p. 21, fig. 87
H. Schiebelhuth, 'Fischlein im Netz', *Stickereien und Spitzen*, 1932–3, pp 12–13

Fig. 57 Madonna and Two Angels, Emmy Zweybrück-Prochaska, Austria, 1934

F2 (NDS 809)

Entitled *Unsere liebe frau* (My beloved lady). Satin with satin appliqué, embroidered with silks and metal threads in cross, four-sided, lazy daisy, stem, satin stitches, couching with gold work and beads. 12¼ × 9¼in. (31 × 23.5cm)

Zweybrück (died 1956) was recognised internationally with frequent reviews in *The Studio*, *Die Kunst*, *Deutsche Kunst und Dekorative*, *Stickereien und Spitzen* and later the *Design* journal. In 1931 she was invited to give a series of lectures at Columbia University, at the Metropolitan Museum, New York, and in Louisville, Kentucky, as well as a two-week course at Willesbare,

Pennsylvania. This was repeated in 1938. She was invited to lecture in Scotland in 1937 but after protracted negotiations she declined and emigrated to America in 1939.

In her thesis, Heffernan fully discusses Zweybrück's career and work noting a change in style from 1934 when her work becomes ecclesiastical and fascist in appearance. Zweybrück was appointed to Coats AG mill, in 1934, and her embroidery atelier was commissioned to produce designs for promotional purposes at trade exhibitions. Elsi Kay Khöler and Käte Luise Rosenstock may have produced these at Zweybrück's Viennese atelier under her supervision. These pieces would eventually have passed into the NDSS collection.

LITERATURE
NDS, *Contemporary Embroideries*, illus. no. 7, 1938 (*see* Bibliography)
Other works by Zweybrück acquired by the NDS are held in the collections of Duncan of Jordanstone College of Art, University of Dundee; Gray's School of Art, University of Aberdeen; and the National Museums of Scotland, Edinburgh.

Fig. 58 Child's tunic, Bosnia, early 20th century
F54 (NDS 1400)
Cotton, sleeveless with side seams, hem and neck decorated with embroidery in cross, chain, whip and buttonhole stitches. Tasselled braid belt and a button and loop neck fastening. 21in. (53cm) long

Figs 59 & 59a (detail) Teacloth, possibly Denmark, 20th century
F11 (NDS 665)
Hedebo embroidery, pulled and drawn work on linen with satin and chain stitches in stylised flower and plant forms. It is not known if this is original or a copy done in Coats studio. 38¼ × 36¾in. (97 × 93cm)

Originating in the mid 18th century to the west of Copenhagen this type of embroidery relies for its effect on changes of texture and was used for decorating shirt collars and wristbands as well as household goods. Its most distinctive feature is the squares of satin stitch known as kloster blocks

LITERATURE
The Essential Guide to Embroidery, Murdoch Books, 2002, p. 92

Figs 60 & 60a (detail) *Pietà*, designed by Professor Hanne-Nüte Kämmerer, Münster, Germany, 1934
F12 (NDS 747)

White lawn with white cotton shadow work and French knots. The quotation reads 'Dann sol ches ist ge schehen auf dass die schrifterfuellet wuerde' (then it came to pass, so that the word would be fulfilled). 37 × 26in. (94 × 66cm)

This work was inspired by the Hungertuch Lenten hangings which were a popular source at the Schule für Handwerk und Kunstegewerbe. Heffernan points out that at a time when imagery was constrained such religious depictions were at odds with the political regime but that they are being used as oblique references to the artists' and students' political and social concerns.

LITERATURE
NDS, *Contemporary Embroideries*, 1938 (*see* Bibliography)

Figs 61 & 61a **Foal and calf designed and worked by Suse Sandeman-Bermuth, Berlin, 1934**

F13 & 14 (NDS 532, 740)

9 × 9½in. (23 × 24cm)

A similar piece depicting a fawn is in the collection of Duncan of Jordanstone College of Art, University of Dundee. All these small pieces may originally have been part of a larger work similar to that illustrated in Hans Schiebelmuth article 'Landliches Gedicht', *Stickereien und Spitzen*, 1930–31

Figs 62 & 62a (detail) *The Twelve Apostles* **(Last Supper), Münster, Germany, 1934–5**

F15 (NDS 737)

Silk embroidered with silk, black cotton and metal threads in cross, four-sided, running, back, fly, satin stitches, couching and French knots. Designed by Professor Hanne-Nüte Kämmerer and worked by students of the Stadt Schule für Handwerk und Kunstegewerbe. 28 × 13in. (71 × 33cm)

In her thesis, Heffernan points out that the stylised figures and text are similar to those on the Hungertuch (Hunger cloth) Lenten cloth also made by the Münster school in the late 1920s. This was inspired by the 1623 Hungertuch Lenten hangings in Telgte, near Münster, that were hung from Ash Wednesday until Easter Saturday.

Fig. 63 **Stole, Münster, Germany, 1930s**

F17 (NDS 674)

Worked by students of the Stadt Schule für Handwerk und Kunstegeberbe. Embroidery on white silk woven with a spot motif. 92 × 4in. (233.8 × 10cm)

In her thesis, Heffernan suggests that the naive figures are typical of the school's increasing concern with simplification and abstraction and that such modernism also indicates a radical approach to a traditional subject. The figures are combined with emblems and the words 'das wort bei gott und' and 'um anfang war das wort' (art by the word of God).

Other works from the Stadt Schule acquired by the NDS are held by the National Museum of Scotland, Edinburgh; and Gray's School of Art, Robert Gordon University, Aberdeen.

Fig. 64 *St Francis*, **designed and worked by Käte Luise Rosenstock, Leipzig, mid 1930s**

F18

Darned net. 27¼ x23¼in. (69 × 59cm)

In her thesis, Heffernan suggests that Rosenstock, whose designs feature regularly in German Journals from 1925 and *The Needlewoman* in 1935, was possibly a Jewish exile in Britain and may have been employed at the National Needlework Bureau, London. Rosenstock was a friend of Kay Köhler, also from Leipzig, who was appointed as the first 'expert-in-charge' of the Needlework Development Scheme in 1946.

Several other works by Rosenstock are in the NDS collections of the National Museum of Scotland, Edinburgh and Victoria and Albert Museum, London

Fig. 65 Part of a skirt border, Crete, late 18th century

F9 (NDS 5031)

Linen with silk embroidery, mainly Cretan stitch. 13½ × 21½in. (34 × 54.5cm)

Characteristic motifs include a large vase of flowers with a pair of birds, derived from the eastern Tree of Life pattern and the double tailed mermaid from Italy. Carnations, scrolls and scattered animal and bird motifs create a rich effect.

LITERATURE
Needlework Development Scheme, *A Review of the Aims and Activities of the Needlework Development Scheme*, Needlework Development Scheme, Glasgow, 1960

Fig. 66 Mat, Cyprus, 1920/30s

F10 (NDS 194)

Needle-made lace in buttonhole stitch. This rather stiff lace produced mainly for tourists was derived from Italian reticella lace. 12¾ × 18½in. (32.5 × 47cm)

LITERATURE
The Essential Guide to Embroidery, Murdoch Books, 2002, p. 125

Fig. 67 Fragment, Greek Islands, possibly Samos

F21 (NDS 1377)

Silks and metal thread on linen. Floral design of stylised roses and carnations. 12½ × 10in. (32 × 25.5cm)

LITERATURE
Needlework Development Scheme, *A Review of the Aims and Activities of the Needlework Development Scheme*, Needlework Development Scheme, Glasgow, 1960

Fig. 68 Runner, Greece , Northern Sporades, 20th century

F23 (NDS 1368)

Linen embroidered with bird motifs worked in silk threads in satin stitch, with a knotted silk fringe. 34½ × 17½in. (87.5 × 44.5cm)

Fig. 69 **Fragment, Dodecanese, Rhodes**

F24

Heavy evenly woven linen embroidered with thick silk threads in cross stitch. Possibly from a bed tent. 26 × 12in. (66 × 30.5cm)

Fig. 70 **Part of a sleeve, Greek Islands, possibly Chios**

F27

Heavy linen with a stylised tree design embroidered with dyed horsehair in straight stitches with a chain stitched edge. 16½in. (42cm) long

Figs 71 & 71a (detail) **Altar hanging, Amsterdam, Netherlands, 1937**

F28

Cloth of gold with appliquéed metallic fabrics and net, couched gold and silver thread and gold fringe. Central figure of Christ and John the Baptist surrounded by angels making music and symbolic lambs, peacock, river and fish below. The banner reads: 'Omnis Spiritus Laudet Dominum' and was inspired by Psalm 150. 88 × 58in. (223 × 147.5cm)

Fig. 72 **Man's Shirt, Hungary, late 19th century**

F30 (NDS 365)

Cotton with traditional black woollen cross stitch embroidery and drawn thread work, with a few remaining sequins on the sleeves. The cuffs are trimmed with linen lace. Acquired from the *Isabella* home industry Budapest. 18in. (45.7cm) long

LITERATURE

Mary Eirewen Jones, *A History of Western Embroidery*, London, Studio Vista, 1969

Fig. 73 **Apron, Portugal, early 20th century**

F40 (NDS 1075)

Closely woven red wool on a white warp with geometric patterns in loom embroidery (an extra weft has been pulled up in loops on the surface), braid waistband and edging. 24½in. (62cm) long

Fig. 74 **Christmas mat designed and worked by Ulla Kockum, Stockholm, 1948**

F31 (NDS 1334)

Cotton embroidery on a cotton ground. The design of this festive cloth is based on snowflakes. 14in. (35.5cm) square

In 1948 Ulla Kockum was appointed 'expert in charge' at NDS.

LITERATURE

Ulla Kockum (as Ulla Kockum-Øverengen), *Embroideries of Sweden* (see Bibliography), 1952

Fig. 75 Towel scarf, Turkey

F52 (NDS 3321)

Handwoven silk, the ends embroidered with stylised flower motifs in silk and metal threads, tasselled fringe. Carnations, roses and hyacinths were favourite flowers that appear frequently in Turkish embroidery. 84 × 17½in. (215 × 44.5cm)

Fig. 76 Towel scarf, Turkey

F53 (NDS 1243)

Formal tree design in silk and metal threads in pattern darning, with a crochet edging, known as *oya*. 58 × 18in. (147.5 × 46cm)

Fig. 77 Printed textile sample, Marimekko, Finland, 1951–1977

GB1694

13in. (33cm) long. In addition to textile samples the archive also holds catalogues of Marimekko's textile range c1970 and photographs of fabric samples.

Marimekko Textile Company, was established in 1951 by Armi and Viljo Ratia to produce textiles, clothing and accessories. The company rose to international prominence during the 1960s but was taken over by the Amer Group plc in 1985.

Fig. 78 Border of a shawl, Kashmir, 19th century

F31 (NDS 1334)

Cone motifs embroidered in floss silk threads on a fine wool ground. 18½ × 22½in. (47 × 57cm)

Fig. 79 Four narrow, shawl borders, Indian, late 18th or early 19th century

Acc. 134

Silk brocade with silver gilt thread woven in the *minakari* style produced in southern Rajasthan and central India. Sizes approx. 6 × 1½in. (15 × 4cm)

One sheet from a collection of nine sheets of border fragments.

Fig. 80 Hem of a skirt, Sindh, Pakistan or Kutch, Gujarat, early 20th century

F36 (NDS 141)

Coarse cotton ground, tie dyed and embroidered with silk threads and *shisha* work. 19 × 106½in. (48 × 270cm)

Fig. 81 Woman's shawl (*phulkari*), Punjab, now Pakistan, early 20th century

F35 (NDS 1621)

Loosely woven cinnamon coloured cotton (*khaddar*) embroidered with floss silk in surface darning stitch. 100 × 55in. (254 × 140cm)

Traditionally embroidered as trousseau or dowry gifts, the finest phulkari (*phu* means flower) are known as *bagh* or garden, with the stylised floral motifs so densely worked that they completely cover the ground fabric.

Fig. 81a Detail of phulkari

The embroidery is worked from the back so skilfully that almost all the thread is on the front of the work.

Fig. 82 Chinese twelve symbol dragon robe (ch'i-fu), 19th century

F8

Yellow silk embroidered in long and short, satin and stem stitches with couched gold and silver thread. 52⅓in. (133.3cm) long

The dragon was the symbol of imperial authority and four-claw dragon robes (*mang*) such as this were worn by lesser nobles and high court officials. Only the emperor and his immediate family wore five-claw dragon robes. The dragons are in cloud-filled skies above waves and mountains with signs for good luck and longevity such as the bat, crane, swastika, peony and lotus flowers. The twelve ancient traditional symbols incorporated in the design were associated with the authority of the emperor. They are the Sun, Moon, Stars, Mountains, Dragons, Pheasant, Bronze Cups of Sacrifice, Water weed, Grain, Fire, the Ax and the Fu.

Fig. 82a Detail of dragon robe

The stylised flames indicate mythical creatures and above the dragon is the symbol for the Stars representing the eternal unity of sun, moon and earth. At the bottom right is the *Ax*, a symbol of the emperor's power to punish. On the left is the geometrical symbol the *Fu*, derived from the ancient character for happiness.

Fig. 1 **Flower motif, late 16th century**

GB1 (NDS 1367)

Figs 2 & 2a (detail) **Belt with purse and pincushion, early 17th century**
GB2 (NDS 3932)

Fig. 3 **Whitew-ork sampler, mid 17th century**
GB3 (NDS 100)

Figs 4 & 4a (detail) **Embroidered picture, dated 1652**

GB4 (NDS 4105)

LIVERPOOL JOHN MOORES UNIVERSITY
LEARNING SERVICES

Figs 5 & 5a (detail) **Sampler, signed AB or RB 1669**

GB5 (NDS 899)

Fig. 6 **Chair seat, Scottish, late 17th
or early 18th century**

GB6 (NDS 515)

Figs 7 & 7a (detail – see page 18) **Embroidered
and quilted bedcover, early 18th century**

GB12 (NDS 1058)

Fig. 8 **Fragment of embroidery, early 18th century**

GB9 (NDS 3933)

Fig. 9 **Baby's shirt, 18th century**

GB11 (NDS 1391)

Fig. 10 **Part of an apron, early 18th century**

GB8 (NDS 4106)

Fig. 11 Man's waistcoat, late 18th century
GB15 (NDS 124)

Fig. 12 Man's waistcoat, late 18th century

GB16 (NDS 1311)

Fig. 13 **Fragment of a border, early 19th century**
GB23 (NDS 1547)

Fig. 14 **Corner of a handkerchief, early 19th century**
GB27 (NDS 1707)

Fig. 15 Woman's apron c1820s

GB20

LIVERPOOL JOHN MOORES UNIVERSITY
Aldham Robarts L.R.C.
TEL 0151 231 3701/3634

Fig. 16 **Panel for a pole screen, c1830**

GB25 (NDS 5264)

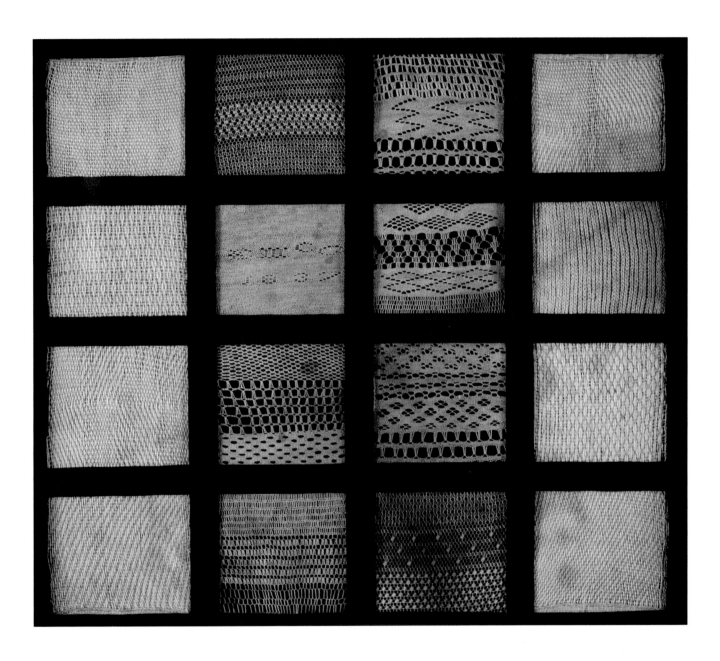

Fig. 17 **Samples of lace filling stitches, signed: E McG 1837**

GB26

Figs 18, 18a & 18b (details)
**Baby robe, Ayrshire work,
mid 19th century**
GB28

Fig. 19 **Baby's bonnet,
Ayrshire work c1862**

GB32 (NDS 1276)

57

LIVERPOOL JOHN MOORES UNIVERSITY
LEARNING SERVICES

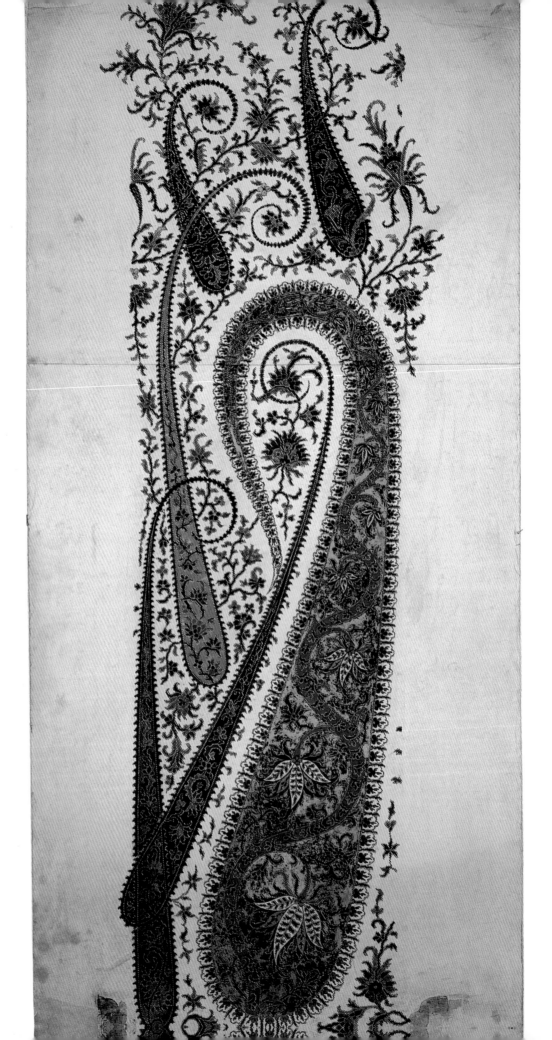

Figs 20 & 20a **Two designs for block printed shawls 1840s–50s**

DC39

Fig. 21 **Tea cosy made by Miss Robertson, Glasgow, 1880s**
GSAT 103

Fig. 22 **Banner designed by Walter Crane, worked by
his wife Mary Frances Crane, 1893**
GSAT 437

Fig. 23 **Mantel border, designed by Jessie Newbery, worked by her aunt, Edith Rowat, mid 1890s**

GB43 (GSAT 441)

Fig. 24 **Cushion cover designed by Jessie Newbery, worked by Edith Rowat, 1890s**

GB42 (GSAT 440)

Fig. 25 **Design for a pulpit fall, Jessie R Newbery c1899**

NMC 006

Fig. 26 **Banner designed by Ann Macbeth, early 1900s**
GSAT 417

Fig. 27 **Triptych, signed and dated: MHP 1903 AD**
GSAT 415

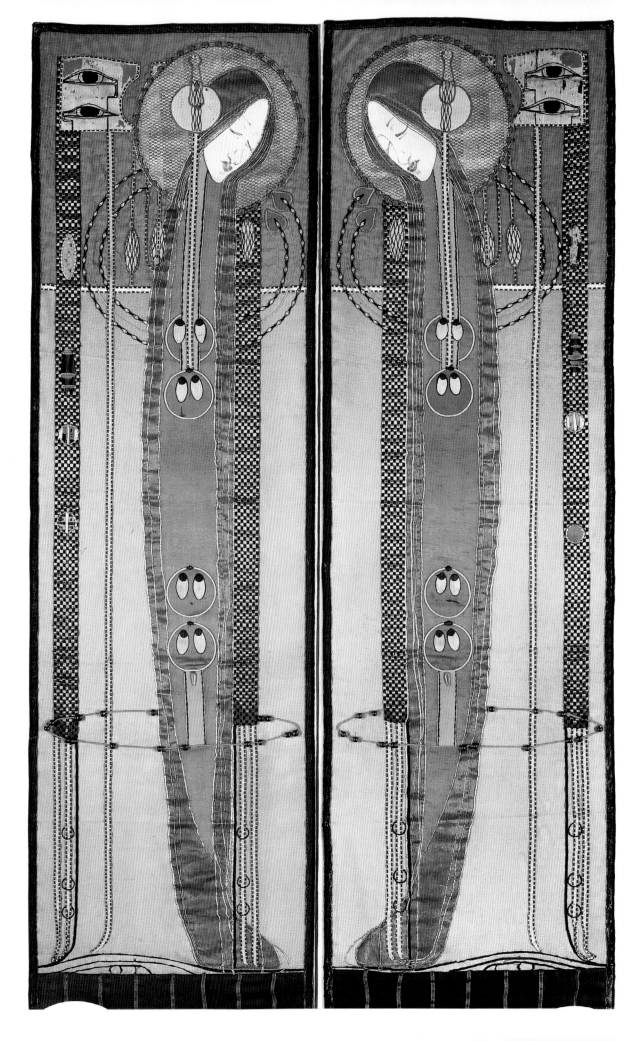

Figs 28 **Pair of panels, designed and worked by Margaret Macdonald Mackintosh, c1904–8**

MC A1a&b

Fig. 29 **Bible markers, possibly designed and worked by Ann Macbeth, c1908–14**

GSAT 421

Fig. 30 **Dress designed and made by Daisy McGlashan,** *c*1910

GSAT 472

Fig. 31 **Collar designed and worked by Grace Melvin,** *c*1912

Acc. 132

68

Figs 32 & 32a (detail) **Panel:** *Carnival*, **designed and worked by Molly Booker,
signed and dated 1932**

GB50 (NDS 301)

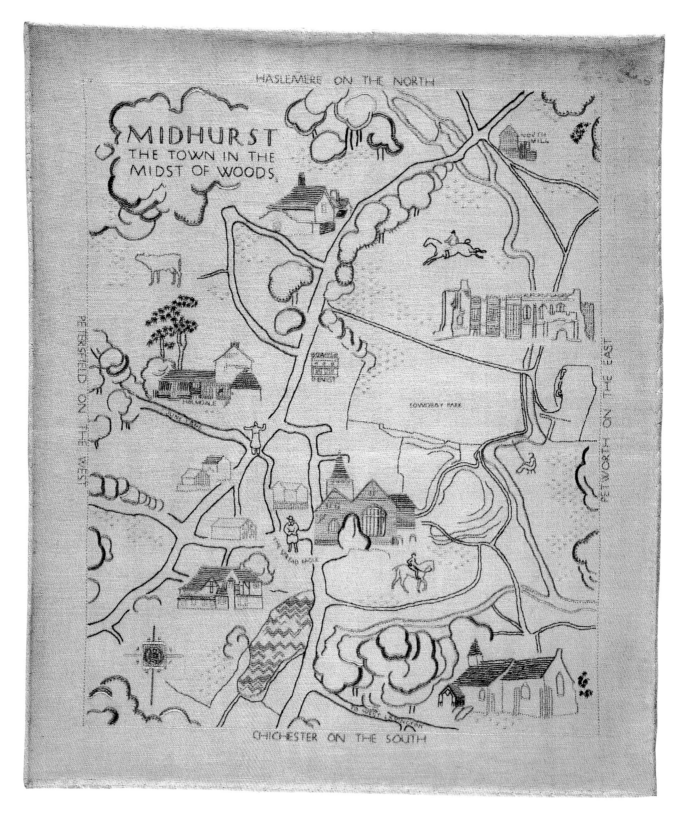

Fig. 33 Map: Midhurst the town in the midst of the woods, mid 1930s
GB53 (NDS 796)

Fig. 34 **Handkerchief sachet designed by Rebecca Crompton, 1938**

GB57 (NDS 407)

Fig. 35 **Teacosy designed by Rebecca Crompton 1938**
GB56 (NDS 416)

Fig. 36 **Missal cover designed and worked
by Joan Mary Nicholson, 1950**
GB61 (NDS 2910)

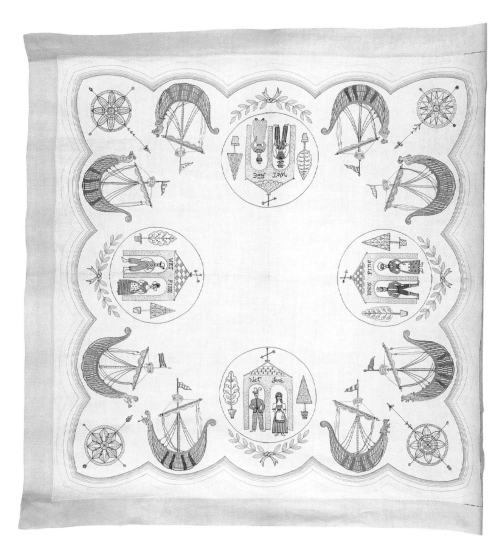

Fig. 37 & 37a (detail) **Nursery tablecloth:
Weather House, 1947**

GB59 (NDS 1351)

LIVERP... ...MOORES UNIVERSITY
LEARNING SERVICES

Fig. 38 **Panel: Hebridean Village c1950**

A2 (NDS 4799)

Fig. 39 **Experimental panel, designed and machine embroidered by Robert Stewart, 1950**

GB63 (NDS 2955)

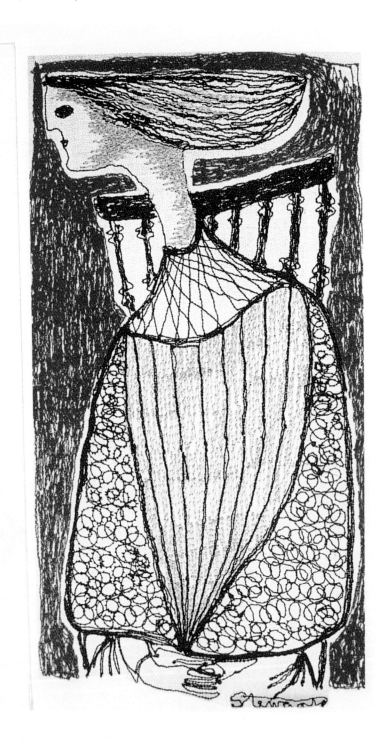

Fig. 40 **Design for embroidery by Robert Stewart, 1950**

Acc. 37

Figs 41 & 41a **(detail of the back of the cushion) Cushion cover designed
by Robert Stewart, worked by Kathleen Whyte, 1951**
GB63 (NDS 2939)

Fig. 42 **Doll representing the novelist Walter Scott c1956**

DC38

Fig. 43 **Dolls representing the painter Allan Ramsay (1713–84) and his second wife Margaret Lindsay, c1956**

DC38

Fig. 44 **Sampler designed by Geraldine White, worked by Beryl Dean, 1958**

GB68 (NDS 5056)

Fig. 45 **Decorative animal made by Shirley Tweedale, Rochdale Grammar School, Greater Manchester, 1959**

GB70 (NDS 5165)

Fig. 46 **Tablecloth designed and worked by Pat Miller, 1960**

GB71 (NDS 5277)

Fig. 47 *Apples*, designed and made by Mary Gribble, mid 1970s
DC29

Fig. 48 **Panel: *Stitch Tree*, designed and worked by Kathleen Whyte, 1977**

DC29

LIVERPOOL JOHN MOORES UNIVERSITY
LEARNING SERVICES

Fig. 49 **Panel designed and worked by Emma Robertson, 1985**
DC29

Fig. 50 **Sample Book, c1930s**

DC37/4/57

Fig. 51 **Shetland shawl, c late 1870s**
EWT TC1/11

Fig. 52 **Knitting sampler, mid 19th century**

Acc. 133

Fig. 53 **Doll's dress and baby cap, designed and worked by Mary Medlam, c1950–80s**

Acc. 133

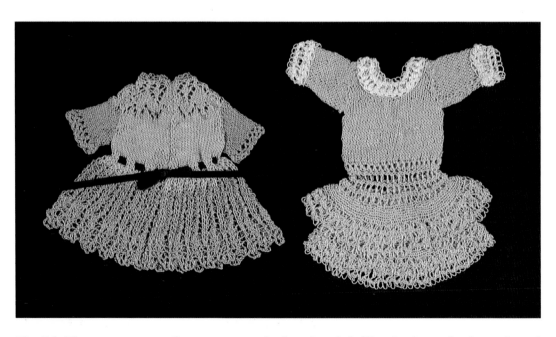

Fig. 54 **Two garments from a sample book of doll's clothes, designed and made by Mary Medlam, c1950–80s**

Acc. 133

Fig. 55 **Circular table cover, Austrian or German, 1920s**
F19

Fig. 56 **Circular table cover Emmy Zweybrück-Prochaska, Austria, late 1920s**

F20 (NDS)

Fig. 57 **Madonna and Two Angels, Emmy Zweybrück-Prochaska, Austria, 1934**

F2 (NDS 809)

Fig. 58 **Child's tunic, Bosnia, early 20th century**

F54 (NDS 1400)

Figs 59 & 59a (detail) **Teacloth, possibly Denmark, 20th century**

F11 (NDS 665)

Figs 60 & 60a (detail) *Pietà*, designed by
**Professor Hanne-Nüte Kämmerer,
Münster, Germany, 1934**
F12 (NDS 747)

Figs 61 & 61a **Foal and calf designed and worked by Suse Sandeman-Bermuth, Berlin, 1934**

F13 & 14 (NDS 532, 740)

Figs 62 & 62a (detail) *The Twelve Apostles (Last Supper)*, **Münster, Germany, 1934–5**

F15 (NDS 737)

Fig. 63 Stole, Münster, Germany, 1930s

F17 (NDS 674)

Fig. 64 *St Francis*, designed and worked by Käte Luise Rosenstock,
Leipzig, mid 1930s

F18

Fig. 65 **Part of a skirt border, Crete, late 18th century**

F9 (NDS 5031)

LIVERPOOL JOHN MOORES UNIVERSITY
LEARNING SERVICES

Fig. 66 **Mat, Cyprus, 1920/30s**

F10 (NDS 194)

Fig. 67 **Fragment, Greek Islands, possibly Samos**

F21 (NDS 1377)

Fig. 68 Runner, Greece , Northern Sporades, 20th century
F23 (NDS 1368)

Fig. 69 Fragment, Dodecanese, Rhodes
F24

Fig. 70 **Part of a sleeve, Greek Islands, possibly Chios**

F27

Figs 71 & 71a (detail) **Altar hanging, Amsterdam, Netherlands, 1937**

F28

Fig. 72 **Man's Shirt, Hungary, late 19th century**
F30 (NDS 365)

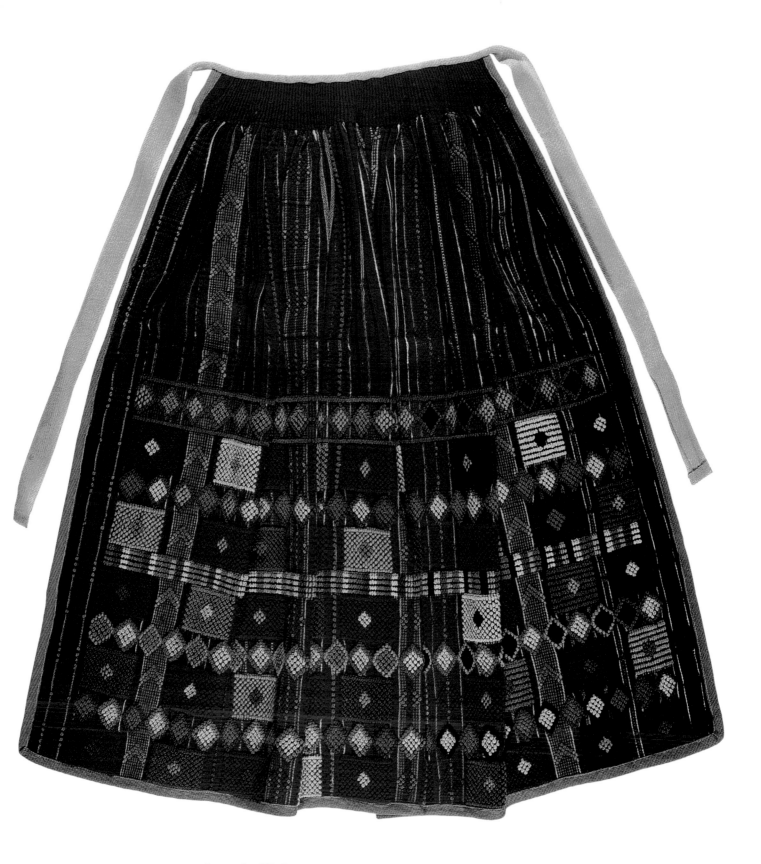

Fig. 73 **Apron, Portugal, early 20th century**

F40 (NDS 1075)

Fig. 74 **Christmas mat designed and worked by Ulla Kockum, Stockholm, 1948**

Fig. 75 Towel scarf, Turkey
F52 (NDS 3321)

LIVERPOOL JOHN MOORES UNIVERSITY
LEARNING SERVICES

Fig. 76 **Towel scarf, Turkey**
F53 (NDS 1243)

Fig. 77 **Printed textile sample, Marimekko,
Finland, 1951–1977**
GB1694

Fig. 78 **Border of a shawl, Kashmir, 19th century**
F31 (NDS 1334)

Fig. 79 **Four narrow, shawl borders, Indian, late 18th or early 19th century**

Acc. 134

Fig. 80 **Hem of a skirt, Sindh, Pakistan or Kutch, Gujarat, early 20th century**

F36 (NDS 141)

Fig. 81 **Woman's shawl (*phulkari*), Punjab, now Pakistan, early 20th century**

F35 (NDS 1621)

Fig. 81a **Detail of phulkari**

LIVERPOOL JOHN MOORES UNIVERSITY
LEARNING SERVICES

Fig. 82 **Chinese twelve symbol dragon robe (ch'i-fu), 19th century**

F8

Fig. 82a **Detail of dragon robe**

Bibliography

Books by staff of the Embroidery Department

Anne Knox Arthur, *An Embroidery Book*, London, 1920

Hannah Frew, *see* Hannah Frew Paterson

Ann Macbeth, *The Playwork Book*, London, 1918
  and Margaret Spence, *School and Fireside Crafts*, London, 1920
  Needleweaving, Kendal, 1922
  Embroidered Lace and Leatherwork, London, 1924
  The Countrywoman's Rug Book, Leicester, 1929

Kathleen Mann, *Peasant Costume in Europe*, Book 1, London, 1931
  Peasant Costume in Europe, Book 2, London, 1936
  Embroidery Design and Stitches, London, 1937
  Appliqué Design and Method, London, 1937
  Designs from Peasant Art, London, 1939
  China Decoration, London, 1952

Hannah Frew Paterson, *Three-Dimensional Embroidery*, London, 1975
  Embroiderer, Glasgow, 1990

Margaret Swanson and Ann Macbeth, *Educational Needlecraft*, London, 1911

Margaret Swanson, *Needlecraft in School*, London, 1916
  Needlecraft for Older Girls, London, 1920
  Needlecraft and Psychology, London, 1926

Kathleen Whyte, *Design in Embroidery*, London, 1969

Other publications

Ancient and Modern Embroidery and Needlecraft, Glasgow, 1916

Liz Arthur, *Kathleen Whyte Embroiderer*, London, 1989
  The Unbroken Thread: A Century of Embroidery & Weaving at Glasgow School of Art, Glasgow, 1994
  Robert Stewart, Design 1946–95, London, 2003

Nasreen Askari and Liz Arthur, *Uncut Cloth, Saris, Shawls and Sashes*, London, 1999

Thomasina Beck, *The Embroiderer's Story, Needlework from the Renaissance to the Present Day*, Newton Abbot, 1995

ed. Jude Burkhauser, *Glasgow Girls: Women in Art and Design 1880–1920*, Edinburgh, 1990

ed. Elizabeth Cumming, *Glasgow 1900, Art & Design*, Amsterdam, Van Gogh Museum, 1933

Mary Hogarth, *Modern Embroidery*, London, 1933

Constance Howard, *Twentieth-Century Embroidery in Great Britain to 1939*, London, 1981

   Twentieth-Century Embroidery in Great Britain 1940–1963, London, 1983

   Twentieth-Century Embroidery in Great Britain 1964–1977, London, 1984

   Twentieth-Century Embroidery in Great Britain from 1977, London, 1986

Pauline Johnstone, *Greek Island Embroidery*, London, 1961

   Three Hundred Years of Embroidery 1600–1900, Treasures from the Collection of the Embroiderers' Guild of Great Britain, East Molesey, 1986

Mary Kessel, *Experiment in Embroidery Design*, Glasgow, 1950

Ulla Kockum-Øverengen, *Embroideries of Sweden from the Collection of the Needlework Development Scheme*, Glasgow, 1950

Needlework Development Scheme, *Contemporary Embroideries. Illustrating some of the works belonging to the collection acquired by the four central art institutions of Scotland under a scheme for the development of needlework in Scotland*, London and Glasgow, Collins, 1938

   Needlework Development Scheme: An Account of its Origin and Aims, Glasgow, 1948

   And So to Embroider bulletins, Glasgow, 1950–60

   A Review of the Aims and Activities of the Needlework Development Scheme, Glasgow, 1960

J. L. Nevinson, 'Needlework in the Home in the Times of Queen Elizabeth and James I', *Embroidery*, September 1936, pp 80–81

R. Oddy, *Embroideries from Needlework Development Scheme*, Edinburgh, Royal Scottish Museum, 1965

Margaret Swain, *Figures on Fabric*, London, 1980

   Scottish Embroidery, London, 1986

   Embroidered Stuart Pictures, Shire Album no. 246, 1990

ed. Lanto Synge, *The Royal School of Needlework Book of Needlework and Embroidery*, London, 1986

Naomi Tarrant, *Textile Treasures, An Introduction to European Decorative Textiles for Home and Church in the National Museums of Scotland*, Edinburgh, 2001

J. Taylor, 'The Glasgow School of Embroidery', *The Studio*, vol. 50, pp 124–35

Catalogues

Elizabeth Cumming, *Glasgow 1900, Art & Design*, Amsterdam, Van Gogh Museum, 1993

F. Macfarlane, and E. Arthur, *Glasgow School of Art Embroidery 1894–1920*, Glasgow, Glasgow Museums and Art Galleries, 1980

Index

LIVERPOOL JOHN MOORES UNIVERSITY
LEARNING SERVICES

LIVERPOOL JOHN MOORES UNIVERSITY
Aldham Robarts L.R.C.
TEL 0151 231 3701/3634